761 Aubert Avenue

761 Aubert Avenue

✦

My Greek American Sanctuary

Second Edition

Jennie C. Vlanton

761 Aubert Avenue
My Greek American Sanctuary

Copyright © 2006 Jennie Vlanton.

iUniverse books may be ordered through booksellers or by contacting:

iUniverse
1663 Liberty Drive
Bloomington, IN 47403
www.iuniverse.com
844-349-9409

Because of the dynamic nature of the Internet, any web addresses or links contained in this book may have changed since publication and may no longer be valid. The views expressed in this work are solely those of the author and do not necessarily reflect the views of the publisher, and the publisher hereby disclaims any responsibility for them.

Any people depicted in stock imagery provided by Getty Images are models, and such images are being used for illustrative purposes only. Certain stock imagery © Getty Images.

ISBN: 978-0-5954-1045-3 (sc)
ISBN: 978-0-5958-5405-9 (e)

Print information available on the last page.

iUniverse rev. date: 02/26/2022

Dedicated to My Parents
Stefan Constantinides and Evangelia Glitsos Constantinides

Contents

Acknowledgements

I would like to acknowledge the encouragement I received, the faith in my ability, and the devotion provided to me by my husband Elias, my daughter Evangeline Newton, and my son Elias. Without their confidence I could never have achieved my goal.

Introduction

As I reflect upon the years of my childhood, questions flood my mind. Why do I feel I have to express my childhood on paper?

Is this a story that has to be told? A story about a unique way of life that brought the best virtues of family and ethnic community into existence.

What were the circumstances that molded my character? The unspoken feeling of unity. The members of the family sharing that unspoken goal. The solidarity of the family.

Who were these people who shaped my life? Parents who came as visitors to the United States but were forced to remain in this country by political circumstances that erupted thousands of miles away. Parents who raised a family under good and difficult times. A family life strengthened by love, unity, traditions and customs.

Where did the ethnic environment exist; an ethnic community that fostered understanding, self-esteem, compassion. Was it on Aubert Avenue, surrounded by Greek American children who lived on the same street, playing with them, going to American and Greek school, participating in other activities with them?

How could an ethnic community have a positive influence on my life? Could these associations have contributed to my self-confidence, knowing that I was surrounded by children who were like me, second generation Greek-American, protected from the prejudice of those who were against foreigners? That besides family life, there was a community where I was liked, wanted, secure, not agitated?

Why are these memories embedded in my mind, happy, nostalgic memories, a part of my collective self?

As I look back upon the years of my childhood, I feel I was very fortunate to be blessed with wonderful parents, people of good character. The virtuous qualities they possessed and passed on to me molded my life. The work ethic they possessed. Their religious beliefs that helped mold the life of my siblings and myself. They worked hard and strenuously to achieve an average way of life, but they surpassed it by their achievement, not only did they survive but they prospered. Hopefully I have been able to pass on this quality of my life to my children, and on their part, to their children.

I also feel fortunate and blessed to have grown up in an ethnic community that gave me self-confidence, security, and many happy memories. In the friendships I made during those early years, there was a bonding and understanding taking place that unconsciously gave me a place in the world. I am proud of the Greek American friends who helped shape my character.

Emigrants arrive in Ellis Island, New York.

1919: Arrival

The S/S Themistocles steamed out of the port of Piraeus, Greece on October 30, 1919. Thirty-five days later, the ocean liner sailed past the impressive Statue of Liberty. The majestic steamship arrived at its destination, the harbor of New York City, on December 4, 1919.

The manifest of the second class passenger list contained the names of Stefan and Evangelia Glitsos Constantinides. Unlike the vast majority of immigrants coming to this country to make this land their permanent home, Stefan and Evangelia were traveling to the United States for their honeymoon. The newlywed couple had planned to stay in the United States for only a short period of time. Their plans included going to St. Louis to visit Evangelia's sister Katina and her husband George Falkedes; her brother John and his wife Irini; and her brother Demo. Then they were to return to Smyrna, Asia Minor to make their permanent home.

After a romance of three years in Smyrna, Stefan and Evangelia became engaged to be married despite objections from Stefan's mother who would have preferred a bride with an expensive dowry. The young couple decided to go to Greece for the marriage ceremony. Since Evangelia's father was dead, and she had no older brothers still living in Smyrna to chaperon the bride, it is said that Fotis Arvanitou, the husband of Evangelia's sister Marianthe, escorted the young couple for the trip across the Aegean Sea from Smyrna to Piraeus, Greece.

Stefan and Evangelia were married on October 2, 1919 in a church in Piraeus. The certificate of their marriage had the stamp of the Church of Saint Spiridon. It reads as follows: *I certify my signature at the bottom certifies as a priest of the Church of Saint Spiridon and under the number 1103 from the second of the month of October, and under the church authority of the Metropolis of Athens, I married Stefan Constantinides and Evangelia Konstantinou Glytsou the day of 2, October 1919. Date certificate issued October 4, 1919 from the clergy in charge Emanuel Mantzouraiti, Piraeus, Greece. October 14 Notary Public I confirm the authenticity of the signature of the priest Emanuel Mantzouraiti of the Church of Saint Spiridon. Signed: (Name unintelligible) Mayor of Piraeus, October 14, 1919.*

The newly married couple left Piraeus a few weeks later for their honeymoon in the United States. Stefan and Evangelia traveled on the steamship Themistocles in second class passage. On their arrival in New York, they were not obligated to leave the ship to go through Ellis Island for processing to enter this country. Their entrance papers were examined onboard ship. Only third class passengers were processed at Ellis Island. Evangelia stated this fact with pride many times on recounting her entrance into the United States.

According to the *Declaration of Alien About to Depart for the United States* from the American Consulate General of Smyrna, Turkey, on September 24, 1919, Evangelia was a subject of Greece since her birth, and her father and mother were subjects of Greece and were of the Greek race. The Declaration further states that Evangelia gives two references: Michail Ververis, Ottoman Gas Company, Smyrna, the country from which declarant starts; and Yankos Glytchos, 613 No. Broadway, St. Louis, Mo., U.S.A. She states she expects to go to the United States, with the object of her visit to join her brothers and sister as shown by letters received from them as proof of object. She states she will reside at the address stated with her brother Yankos Glytchos of the U.S., whose occupation is shopkeeper. Signed by H. Earle Russell, American Vice Consul.

The ship's manifest states that Fedon Papadakis was the last person to see Stefan and Evangelia as they left Piraeus. Fedon was a brother-in-law to Nick Kassimates. Stefan's family held Russian citizenship, although the family lived in Smyrna, Turkey for generations. In 1795, an ancestor, Simeon Konstantinou, went on business to the city of Taiganion in Russia and obtained Russian citizenship. After that, the name was changed to Konstantinoff. This procedure was common practice by many Greeks who lived in Turkey. Russia had declared she was the protector of all Orthodox people living in that country and therefore people of Greek ancestry felt a measure of comfort in having Russian citizenship. The Russian citizenship was handed down from generation to generation. Stefan and Evangelia entered the United States with Russian citizenship.

Stefan's birth date is April 4, 1887. Stefan's parents, John and Olympia Constantinides, had five children: the oldest child, Maria, then four sons, Demetros, Stefan, George and Platon. Stefan was very well educated, having attended the American school, the Evangeliki College where he was a graduate in accounting. Stefan practiced that profession in Smyrna before coming to the United States. In the book, *The Katacouzinos Family, Voice of the Fatherland* written by Simon Katacouzinos, Olympia's brother and godfather of Stefan, it is stated that the land for the establishment of the Evangeliki College had been donated for the school by an ancestor. Stefan spoke five languages fluently, Greek, English, French, Turkish and Russian.

Evangelia's birth date is January 19, 1898. Her parents, Kostas and Ioanna Zacharias Glitsos, had five children: a daughter Marianthe; a son Demetrios (Demo); a second son John; followed by two daughters, Katina and Evangelia. Joanna died in childbirth with a sixth child, who also died. It has been said by a family member that Ioanna, Evangelia's mother, had been a teacher before her marriage.

Kostas was concerned that his five young children were motherless, so he married Kakouli Hatzipavli. With Kakouli he had three more children: Thomas, Eleni and Vasili, who died in childhood.

Evangelia was educated according to the practice of the times for women. She had the equivalent of a high school education, with the emphasis on sewing. She was a seamstress in Smyrna, and enjoyed mentioning the prominent women who were part of her clientele, among them wives of ambassadors.

Stefan came from a wealthy family. The Constantinides family lived in a suburb of Smyrna called Koukloutza (present day Altindag). His parents were John and Olympia Katacouzinos (Cantacouzinos) Constantinides. The family owned much property. The extensive land holding included an olive still. When the patriarch of the family needed money, he would sell a few parcels of land without feeling much loss in acreage. In the home there was a gun rack used for hunting birds and animals.

In 1973 my son Elias went to Smyrna in search of my father's home in the suburb of Koukloutza. Before my mother died she explained to Elias where the home was located, and what landmarks to look for. Not knowing Turkish, Elias tried to communicate in English and French with a bus driver where he was headed. An elderly man, sitting on the bus, said to him in Greek, "Where do you want to go my child?". He was a Turk who had been born in Crete and went to Turkey during the exchange of populations in 1923. With the help of this kind man, they looked for an area that had nine faucets, which they found on the side of a mosque that had been a monastery. They found the house and there were still Greek letters on the outside. The house was in ruins from the 1922 Catastrophe but a Turkish family was living in two rooms that remained habitable. The house was situated on a hill, with a spectacular view overlooking the city of Smyrna spread below.

Stefan's mother, Olympia, was descended from the Byzantine emperor John Katacouzinos, who reigned in Constantinople from 1347 to 1354. She herself had been born in Trieste, which was a part of the country of Austria at the time of her birth. Olympia's birth occurred in the middle of the nineteenth century. She was a matriarch who ruled her home with a firm hand. She did not approve of the marriage between her son and Evangelia, because she expected the bride to have an impressive dowry, including gold.

Evangelia's family was from the small business middle class in Smyrna. Her grandfather had been a Greek Orthodox priest in Smyrna. Her father, Kostas, at one time entertained the thought of becoming a priest, but was disillusioned when he saw the irreligious behavior of the monks with the nuns and their drinking wine. He went into the restaurant business instead. Evangelia was very proud of the fact that he often brought entertainers from Greece to perform in his establishment.

Kostas' family originally had come from the island of Kythera (Cerigo), although Evangelia did not know any details of the emigrating ancestor or when he had actually emigrated to Smyrna. To this day there are two villages on the island of Kythera, Dokana and Kyprianika, where the predominant families are named Glitsos. In 1995 my son Elias and I visited those two villages, and met many people with the last name of Glitsos.

The Glitsos Family in Smyrna in 1913.

1922: Catastrophe

Stefan and Evangelia arrived in this country with a considerable amount of money and Stefan was eventually able to invest his money in several businesses. However, political events thousands of miles away had a profound effect on their lives. It was called the 1922 Catastrophe of Smyrna.

This human upheaval was brought about by the victorious Allies of World War I. The Great Powers, England, France, the United States and Italy, had promised the Greek government that if Greece entered the war on their side, the city of Smyrna and the western part of Turkey would be awarded to Greece at the end of hostilities.

At the conclusion of World War I, and under the protection of Allied destroyers, Greece landed troops in Smyrna in May, 1919. My brother Platon recalls that our father told him that during those days of the Greek troop landing in Smyrna, he had taken a gun and had gone to the pier. He hid in a doorway, and watched the Greek troops disembark. Johnny says that Dad related to him that a Turkish friend at that time told him trouble was brewing in Turkey and that he should leave the country immediately.

The Allied political agreement brought about monumental and disastrous consequences for the small country of Greece. The result was the massacre of a million Greeks and Armenians. The catastrophe of Smyrna produced a million and a half Greek refugees and saw the annihilation of a Greek presence in Asia Minor after three millennia.

Fortunately, Stefan and Evangelia were still visiting the United States during these critical months. Regrettably, the members of both their families who were still in Smyrna, became refugees. All was lost. Stefan and Evangelia were devastated. Stefan would tell his wife, "Piso, yinneka, piso" (Back, wife, back). She in turn recounted many times how she cried for three days and nights, to return to Smyrna. They wanted to go home to their beloved families and the city they loved in spite of the fact that Stefan's business enterprises were doing very well here.

Without question, to return to Smyrna was no longer an option. In order to help Evangelia adjust to the new realization that they would never be able to return to their homeland, Stefan tried to console his wife by showering her with money. He told her about and showed her how much money he had made from his several businesses. He would say, "Look, yinneka, (wife), look at all the money we are making." However, Evangelia could not be reconciled to the thought of not going back to the city she loved and where she had been born and raised. In spite of the fact that her husband was doing very well financially here, and even though the Catastrophe of Smyrna was irreversible, her desire was to go back to her home.

But Evangelia's and Stefan's fate was sealed. St. Louis, Missouri, United States of America, was to be their home for the rest of their lives. And God blessed them with four loving, beautiful, wonderful children: Olympia, Jennie, Platon and John.

761 Aubert Avenue

Since Stefan's and Evangelia's original intentions were to return to their home-land of Smyrna to live, their first home in St. Louis was a rented one. It was located at 4724a Olive Street in the Central West End, in an upscale neighbor-hood at that time. Their first child, Olympia, was born there.

About 1923, with the obliteration of their hopes of returning to their home-land, and realizing the United States was to be their permanent home now, they decided to buy a home in an adjacent area at 761 Aubert Avenue. In the follow-ing years, their other children, Jennie, Platon and John, were born in that house. My parents owned that house until 1944, when they bought the house at 5021 North Kingshighway Boulevard.

I often wondered about the name of our street, *Aubert.* I wondered where the name came from. I have since learned that the street was named for Jean Louis Aubert, a French writer, who lived from 1731 to 1814. He was a professor of lit-erature in the Royal College and editor of the Gazette de France. The name Aub-ert is on the original plot of the Aubert Place subdivision in 1857. An interesting fact, since St. Louis was originally settled by the French in 1764.

I have many tender feelings for our house on Aubert Avenue. That dwelling holds many memories for me of a carefree, happy childhood. When I was a youngster I used to wonder about the house I was born in. It was a red brick building but one of the things that I noticed about the house was that the bricks were not the same color of red as some of the other houses on the street. Though it was built a few years before the other houses, probably at the turn of the twen-tieth century, it was on a par with any of them.

The house was a two family flat, well built, and solidly constructed like the other homes on the block. In the front of the house there was a long stretch of porch accommodating not only the entrance to the first floor, but also, the entrance to the second floor as well.

I have come to learn to recognize that there are styles in homes just as there are styles in fashions and in automobiles. As well as I can determine, the style of the house was late Victorian. There was no gingerbread molding on the porch or on any part of the house, but there were two gables above the second story that gave the deceptive appearance of a third floor, or possibly an attic. Actually, the gables served merely to alter the appearance of the front of the house and make it look larger than what it really was.

Most of the homes on Aubert had a front lawn terrace. That is, from the street level sidewalk a person had to walk up ten or twelve steps to the yard above. From there, one would walk a few steps to the front porch stairs and then up the five or six steps to the porch.

On the lawn were three mulberry trees, which when they blossomed proclaimed spring had arrived. As children, it was our delight to sample the mulberries until we saw the stains the fruit would leave on our hands and clothes.

In the back of the house were two large, screened-in porches, again one for each floor. On the hot humid nights that St. Louis is well known for, the back porch accommodated the whole family for sleeping.

As I look back upon it now, it was a comfortable house. The rooms were large and spacious. By today's standards it would be classified as too big with too much wasted space and possibly a little awkward. But by the standards of family living, it was very well suited for raising an average sized family. There was room in it to breathe, to think, to romp, to play, to be an individual without getting in anyone else's way. In that house there was space, if the mood suited one, to be a part of the family circle; and then again, if one had the feeling of wanting to be alone, there was space to curl up in one's own ivory tower. One could find a corner without being disturbed, and be alone.

In the backyard with neighbors, 1925.

The Backyard

Although the house was built on a city lot, thirty-five feet wide, there was a depth of two hundred feet all the way back to the alley. One of the pronounced pleasures of the house on Aubert Avenue that recalled many fond memories for me, was the backyard. It was not the typical small city lot. It was deep and level, stretching about a hundred feet from the back of the house to the alley. There was no garage to interfere with the expanse of the backyard.

Both sides of the backyard were fenced in. On the left side facing the yard from the back porch, was a metal cyclone fence. On the right side there was a wooden fence, unpainted, with several loose, rotting boards. On occasion, those boards served as a useful exit and entrance to the house next door, particularly if one of us wanted to talk to or play with any of the children who lived there, Alex or Pete John, or Tula or George Alexandres. We had easy passage, both ways, our house to theirs, or their house to ours. There was a sidewalk along the cyclone fence on the other side of the yard, going all the way down to the three steps leading to the alley.

Every year my father tended with great care the flower garden which ran alongside the length of the sidewalk. The flower garden was long and narrow in shape, hugging the outline of the sidewalk from the beginning of the backyard to the steps leading to the alley. He had a fondness for roses and had planted about twelve rose bushes. Many times my brothers had to dig small gullies around the individual rose bushes so the water could get to each plant. My father never watered his rose bushes by sprinkling over the top of the bush, he laid the hose on the ground and let the water run like a rivulet at the side of the bush's roots.

At the far end of the flower garden beautiful purple iris bloomed. For me it was an unexplained pleasure every spring to see the iris bloom and to enjoy the shape of their petals, which reminded me of exotic orchids. To this day, I can recall the beauty of their vivid color as they blossomed in early Spring.

Midway in the flower garden was a cherry tree which blossomed in late April around the twenty-seventh of the month, on my birthday. I secretly reveled that the blossoming of the tree was a private gift to me.

The cherry tree was periodically attacked by Platon or Johnny who saw the tree as a challenge to be conquered by them. Often several of the slim branches were broken as one of the boys climbed the tree. The branches were not strong enough to withstand the onslaught of an aggressive boy.

From the center of the back yard to the alley, my father planted a vegetable garden. He left a section of the yard available for our tenants, the Laskaris family who rented the upstairs unit of our house. My brothers Platon and Johnny remember well that my mother had them dig the renter's portion of the garden even though the Laskaris family had an older son who was in his late teens. Nick was strong and very capable of that chore, but my mother always tried to accommodate our renters.

One of my parents' favorite vegetables which did very well in the garden and which they used daily in salads was watercress (roka). Relatives in Greece sent them the seeds. As children we did not appreciate the uniqueness of watercress and considered it an odd vegetable, not knowing at the time how expensive and specialized a salad green it really was, one not frequently found at the grocery store among the standard vegetables displayed. The garden also had tomatoes, corn, and zucchini squash.

In those years, Arbor Day was celebrated on April 6. In order to teach children about the preservation of the environment and care of trees in particular, it was customary for the school to give a tree sapling to a child to plant. When I became a teacher, many years later, that practice was still observed. When Platon was in the fourth grade at Washington Elementary School, he was given a Chinese elm sapling at school. He brought it home and with eagerness and vigor, planted it. Platon took great care of it. In no time at all, the sapling took root, and in the following years it grew sturdy and spread its branches. Even after we had moved away from the old neighborhood, when we drove down Kingshighway Boulevard, the street parallel and west of Aubert Avenue, we could still see the backyard and the huge branches of Platon's elm tree. To this day we still refer to it as Platon's tree. It is still a strong and strapping tree, visible from Kingshighway Boulevard!

Another facet of the backyard I recall with pleasure was the grape arbor that my father built. It was next to the back porch. The height of the arbor reached to about eight feet above the ground, level with the entrance to the back porch. My father placed coffee grounds around the roots of the grape plant. He claimed the acid in the grounds was a very good fertilizer.

I enjoyed standing on the porch landing and looking over the top of the grape arbor. It gave me a feeling of being at the top of the world, surveying the magnificence of the cosmos. Another feeling the grape arbor conveyed was one of protection from the outside world. It was with a refreshing feeling to stand in the coolness of its shade, to look above and see among the grape leaves the clusters of dark blue grapes hanging down, beckoning to us. It was a special place to go to with a book, to sit and read, or just to be alone in solitary presence and enjoy the ambiance. No intrusive thoughts. Needless to say, the grape arbor was a favorite place for my siblings also.

In that period of time every home had an ash pit. The ash pit was also at the back end of the yard next to the alley, where the ashes from the coal furnace and other trash that accumulated during the year were deposited. Once a year, always in the summer, the ash pit was emptied. The ash pit had to be empty in time for fall, when the coal furnaces, both upstairs and downstairs, were in use again.

Usually a junkman, white or black, with a horse and wagon or an old worn-out truck would come by and give my mother a price to empty the ash pit. The price was negotiable but I don't recall that my mother ever forcefully negotiated a lower price. I think she felt sorry for the men who had to do that filthy and menial work. The work required two men. They would get in the ash pit with shovels, on top of the trash and ashes, and start digging their way to the bottom, usually encountering a rat or two. Often the job required a whole day to be completed. Sometimes my mother or my father would complain that the men had not shoveled out the ash pit as well as they could, by not going down to the bottom of the pit.

With all those things in the backyard, the cherry tree, the elm tree, the vegetable garden, the flower garden, the grape arbor, the ash pit, there was still a sizable empty space in the middle of the yard. Here, laundry lines were strung from the fences between one side of the yard to the other.

We had a big, straw laundry basket with handles at each end. It usually took two people to carry the basket out, each holding on to a handle. I remember helping my mother with that chore, lugging the basket full of wet clothes. Later, that responsibility fell on my sister and me to do the laundry on Saturday mornings.

Even with the laundry lines, there was still room left in the backyard for a play area. The sidewalk by the porch was wide enough for us to jump rope, try our hand at double dutch, or draw a diagram on the sidewalk with chalk to play hopscotch. On extremely hot days we would put on our bathing suits and run out into the yard, squealing and laughing, as the first spray of water from the hose hit our bodies. These actions alerted inquisitive neighbors to look down from their back porches at our antics as we splashed each other with the water hose. Sometimes we were moved by the moment and held the water hose and did a little quick dance, refreshing ourselves by sprinkling each other with the water.

The back porch stood on posts three feet high. The space underneath it was the ideal place to play when we were little. It was shaded away from the sun, away from the elements. It was finished, paved with cement, and the concrete extended to even under the area of the steps that went up to the porch. Three steps on the side next to the wall led down to the basement. I remember playing there on rainy days with my sister, with our dolls and our doll buggy. I felt so secure and privileged to be able to play outdoors, protected from the rain!

The porch was screened in, and stretched from one end of the house almost to the other. There were canvas awnings that could be rolled up and down to provide for privacy from the neighbors and protection from the rain. The porch was large enough to accommodate the whole family for sleeping outside in the summer. My mother would set up a double bed and also move the day bed from her bedroom that my brothers slept on, to the porch. There was still enough room for a table for us to have our meals.

My brothers recall that everyone in the family slept on the porch except my father. No matter how hot the nights were, he slept in his bedroom.

In the beginning, when my mother started working and before business had picked up at the cleaners, once in a while Platon and I would go down the street to 793 Aubert Avenue to my Uncle Demo's and Aunt Anna's house and play with our cousins Joanna, Marie and Dessie. Later on, when my aunt and uncle moved next door to us, at 759, Platon and Johnny would go over to their house and spend time with their cousins, or to gently antagonize them, as the case may be.

We moved away from Aubert Avenue to 5021 North Kingshighway Boulevard in August 1944, after Olympia and Joe were married in June of that year. As the years pass, my siblings and I still recall happy memories of 761 Aubert Avenue; memories we cherish of an unforgettable childhood.

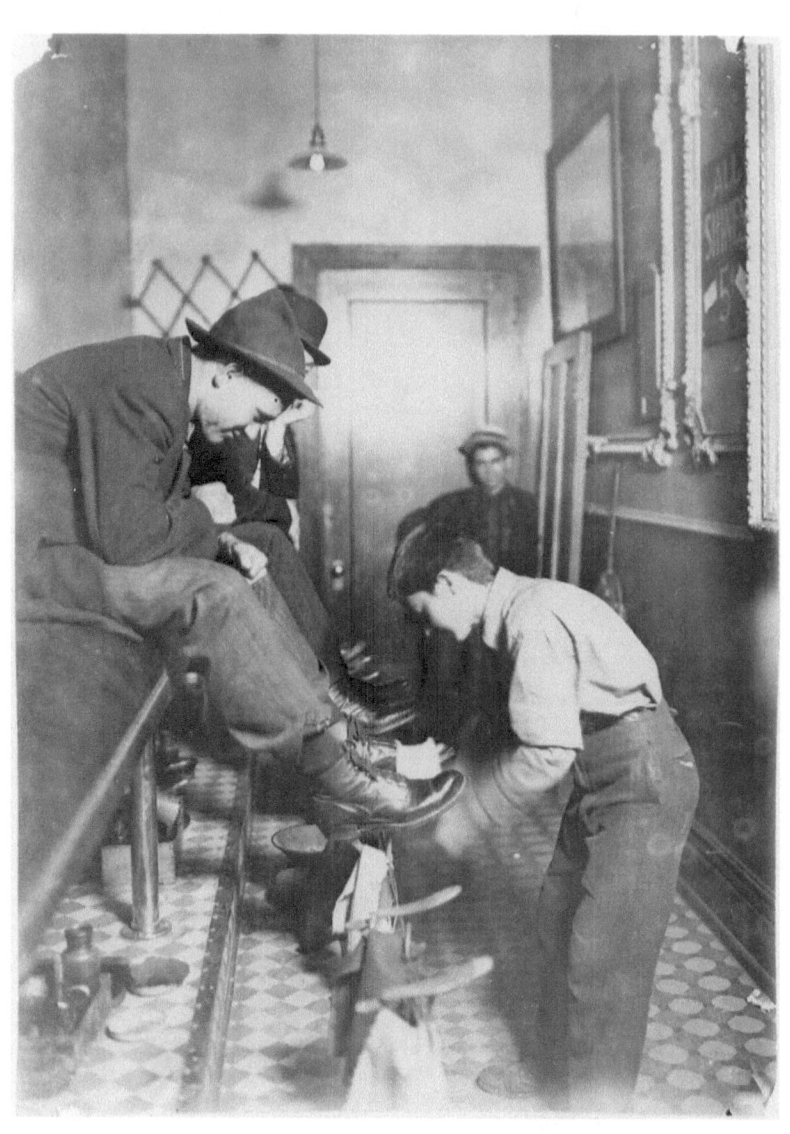

Stefan's Enterprises

At one time in the early 1920's, my father owned three businesses. The first one was the Broadway Shoe Shining Parlor, at 613 North Broadway Boulevard, located in the downtown business district, a few blocks from the Mississippi River and present day Busch Stadium. The parlor was bought from my mother's brother, John Glitsos. The year is not clear when my father bought that store since the St. Louis City Directory of 1920 and 1922 lists John Glitsos as owner, although by that time John had moved with his family and was living in Phoenix, Arizona where his sister, Katina and her family had moved in 1920.

The second business my father had was a dry cleaners and hatters store. In the St. Louis City Directory for the years 1921 and 1922 there is a listing for Stephan Constantinides, shoe polisher at 5881 Delmar Boulevard.

The third business my father was involved with was Progressive Hatters and Cleaners at 4480 Easton Avenue (now Martin Luther King Drive). His partner was Nestor Papaspanos. Later, my father became the sole owner.

Gradually my father sold the first two businesses; he felt with a partner at the Easton Avenue store he had more time for himself and his family.

The shoe shine parlor on Broadway Boulevard he had sold to his brother George. My sister Olympia remembers when she was about fourteen years old, in the Thirties, taking the Hodiamont streetcar east and going downtown to the Broadway store to get money owed to my father for the business. Sometimes, she says, Uncle George bought meat from Union Market on Delmar Avenue and 6th Street and gave her that to bring to my father instead of money. Those were partial payments.

My brother Platon says he also remembers going three times to Uncle George's store on Broadway to shine shoes. The agreement was Platon was to keep the money he earned, but Uncle George took most of the money and gave him very little. When dad found out about the way Uncle George was treating Platon, he forbade him to work for Uncle George anymore.

My father sold the Delmar Avenue store to my mother's brother Demo. It was doing a very good business. Unfortunately, after a few years Demo was forced to close the store, because a competitor, a Greek, opened the American Cleaners directly across the street from him and was able to drive Demo out of business.

Both of these situations took place in the late Twenties or early Thirties.

My father and his partner, Nestor Papaspanos, did very well with the Easton Avenue store. Up until the early Thirties, that business sustained two growing families very well. But I recall that when Johnny (who was born in 1932) was about two years old, the Depression hit. The business at the Easton store went down to almost nothing.

My father and his partner decided to sever the partnership; one to buy the other out. I recall hearing my parents discussing the situation at the time. My father decided he would try to keep the business and buy his partner out. He did not have enough money on hand to pay for the partner's share so he decided to borrow on his life insurance, a John Hancock policy. Thus, Progressive Hatters and Cleaners became his.

The Progressive Cleaners, 1949.

The Magazi

On the large plate glass window store front, in a half circle in gold letters, was the word Progressive, and below in a straight line, Hatters and Cleaners. Progressive Hatters and Cleaners. 4480 Easton Avenue. From the early 1920's on, this enterprise held a meaningful and important place in the life of my family.

To my family it was known as the magazi.

The magazi (the store) was, as my brother Johnny has said, an institution central to the family of Evangelia and her husband Stefan, their children, grandchildren and their relatives. The magazi was an institution, an entity. It was both very demanding and very generous in its benefits. None of the family was immune to the impact of the magazi.

The magazi had a personality all its own, unlike so many other businesses of the time. On entering the store, the wall on the left had mirrors from about two feet off the floor then rising to the ceiling. The frames around all the mirrors were varnished a dark color, almost black mahogany. Further in, by that wall was a pressing machine and the clothes racks that held the cleaned clothes covered by paper bags.

On the opposite side of the store, towards the front, was the hat blocking equipment next to the window. There was a showcase for the hats to be placed in when they were cleaned and blocked.

Next to the showcase was the shoeshine stand. On it were four black chairs with arms that were carved at the ends like animal paws. The back and seat were of black leather. The chairs were set on a marble stand with brass foot pedestals where the customer rested his feet while his shoes were shined. Above the chairs were mirrors, about four feet high, going to the ceiling.

There was another showcase next to the shoeshine stand. This one was about seven feet high and built to specifically hold long evening dresses. Next to the evening dress showcase was a curtained booth, about two feet wide, and three to four feet long, with a chair where a customer sat while his pants was being pressed. This little booth was often occupied on rainy days by people who had gotten their suits or overcoats wet and wanted them pressed right away. The partition separating the front of the store from the back work area had full length mirrors, starting from the floor to about eight feet high.

In the winter when the pressing machine was in use, the window in the front of the store would steam up. No one could see outside, and no one on the outside could look in. I always thought it was kind of funny to see customers who wore glasses come into the store and immediately have their glasses fog up. They would have to take them off, wipe them, and put them on again before they could transact their business. This always made me secretly smile.

Sense Of Duty

For my father, the magazi meant security, pride, independence. It gave him the satisfaction of knowing he was capable of providing for his family a good living. He knew his family would have food, a roof over their heads, even during the worst period of the Depression. His family would not need to go on public relief or depend on handouts from others.

My father was a kind, compassionate, mild-mannered man. He was a man of refinement, not vulgar. He never insulted or struck or reprimanded his children. Even when Platon and Johnny were horsing around, wrestling, my father would say to them in a joking manner, "You're going to destroy the house."

I can never recall that he ever complained of the long hours he put in at the cleaners. When he had a partner, they had a schedule where they each worked half-days. The magazi was still open thirteen hours a day then, from eight o' clock in the morning to nine o' clock at night. The working day was split into two shifts. One week my father would have the early shift, the next week he would have the late shift.

Once dad bought out his partner and became the sole owner, he put in the full thirteen hours himself. My father would open the magazi promptly at eight in the morning and close at nine in the evening. That was during the week and on Saturdays. He also had the store open Sunday from nine in the morning to one in the afternoon.

Since the store was not doing well when he bought out his partner, he could not afford to hire any help. He did everything himself, shine shoes, clean and block hats, press clothes. How many times I felt sad watching him shine the shoes of a customer who was sitting on a chair, with his feet on the foot rests. How humiliating, degrading and demeaning for my father to lower his position to shine shoes. It hurt me. My father had dignity, he was too good to have to do that, to be reduced to polishing someone else's shoes. And yet, I never heard him complain about shining shoes, or the long hours he was putting in at the cleaners.

When he got home from the store at nine-thirty in the evening, he would eat dinner. He would stay up for about an hour, and then go to bed. The next morning, when he got up he was always in a good mood. Sometimes he even sang while he shaved. One of his favorite songs was La Donne Mobile from the opera Rigoletto. I recall the first time I had ever heard that song, was hearing my dad sing it, even before I had any idea what an opera was.

Then at seven thirty in the morning, he would leave the house, walk north for half a block on Aubert Avenue to the Hodiamont street car line on his way to the magazi. His duty, his responsibility, were clear to him. There was no question in his mind about his role. He was the head of the family, this was the lifestyle for him. He did it willingly and happily because it sustained and nurtured his family.

In recalling all the years I worked for my father, I am amazed he never once yelled at me or corrected me, or said anything cross or embarrassed me. He was always a gentleman. He might become perturbed or irritated with a customer, but he never said or reacted negatively. He would just light a cigarette and smoke silently. Smoking was his only vice.

Having been an accountant in Smyrna by profession before coming to the United States and becoming a dry cleaner, my father kept accurate and systematic business records. After we bought the house on Kingshighway Boulevard in 1944, the Internal Revenue Service called for an audit of my father's income tax return. This was done often right after World War II, particularly to small business men, to see if they had reported all their income during the war years.

I took his books to the Internal Revenue Service office in the Federal Building in downtown St. Louis, on Market Street. When the auditor looked at the order and neatness of the books, he commented how well the books were kept. Even though the ledger was kept in Greek, the auditor, after skimming over several pages, told me the audit was over. He was satisfied that everything was complete and in order, and I left the office.

Stefan and Evangelia with Olympia, 1923.

Lifeline

For my mother, the magazi was everything. It was her lifeline. It meant financial security. It meant prestige to her in her circle of friends. Among the seventeen Greek families where we lived on Aubert Avenue, her husband was the most successful. He owned his own store, a successful enterprise. He was in business for himself. He was not a salaried employee, working for someone else. She would often say, "A man who is on a weekly salary cannot achieve financial success." Meaning, a salaried employee cannot begin to compare financially with someone who is in business for himself.

After my father became the sole owner of Progressive Hatters and Cleaners, my mother discussed with him to let her work part time at the magazi doing alterations and mending. I recall he put up some resistance at first. His manner as always was quiet, not loud or virulent, no angry outbursts. Quiet was his way. She insisted on going to work at the cleaners. She prevailed and started working with him.

The magazi gave my mother pride that she was supportive of her husband, and she helped in the business to make it successful. She set an example for several other Greek women whose husbands had cleaners. They started being seamstresses in their husbands' businesses too.

My mother' s hours working at the magazi were not the same as my father's because she still had four children to care for at home, ages 2, 4, 10, and 13. She had a home to manage. Her schedule was to stay at home until 3:30 in the afternoon when my sister and I came home from school. This way she could cook and prepare the meals for the family, do her household chores, and care for my two younger brothers who were still at home.

At 3:30 in the afternoon when my sister and I arrived home from school, my mother would leave for the magazi. She would board the Hodiamont streetcar at the Aubert Avenue stop, go east, get off at Taylor Avenue and transfer going north on the Taylor street car to Easton Avenue. She'd get off and walk past several stores, a shoe store, a dress store, a restaurant, a grocery store, another store which was empty, then 4480, the cleaners. At the cleaners she worked until she and my father closed the store at nine in the evening.

I never heard her complain of all the work she did, or of the responsibility she had.

The Journey Home

There was a store directly across the street from the cleaners with the name Sam the Tailor posted across the plate glass window. It was operated by a husband and wife. It was primarily a tailoring shop but Sam also took in dry cleaning of clothes. Sam' s closing hour in the evening was also nine o' clock, and my parents would never close the store unless Sam closed first. In case a customer would go and find Sam's store closed, our store was open to accommodate the customer. My father was ever observant of Sam' s movements. When there was no longer any light burning in the store across the street, my father would say, "Sam has turned off his lights. He has closed. Now we can close the store too and get ready to go home."

Every evening after closing the cleaners, my father would go into the partitioned back work area of the store where he could be alone. He would stand facing the east, and pray. On several occasions I accidentally protruded on his concentration. When he was finished praying, we would leave. He would lock the front door and make the sign of the cross over the lock.

Before we got our first automobile, we would take the street car home. We would cross the street to the corner of Easton Avenue and Taylor Avenue, take the Taylor streetcar going south, and get off at the Hodiamont street car line to go west. By then it was about 9:15 in the evening. The street car was usually slow in coming at that hour, and on bitter cold nights in the winter, my parents and I huddled in the doorway of the corner drugstore, trying to keep warm from the freezing weather. When the Hodiamont street car finally arrived, we gratefully boarded it and rode to our stop, Aubert Avenue. We'd get off and walk to the middle of the block to 761, home.

During the summer months, the traditionally slow periods in the dry cleaning business, there were many times we walked home from the cleaners, a distance of about three miles. My father, my mother, and I or any other sibling who had been at the cleaners that day, would leave the store at 9 o' clock, and walk home. Regardless if my father had put in thirteen hours of work; regardless of the hours my mother had worked at home and at the cleaners; regardless of the heat and humidity that is found uniquely only in St. Louis weather, we would walk home.

29

Streetcar fares at the time were ten cents for adults and five cents for children twelve years of age or younger. That was a considerable amount of money in the period of the Depression and an amount that could be saved if a person was willing to walk.

When we walked home, we would walk down Taylor Avenue going south to Page Boulevard. We would go west by turning right, walk down about a block to West End Avenue, then to Newberry Terrace, right for several blocks to Walton Avenue, turn left going south for a block to Fountain Park, west again for three blocks to Aubert Avenue, and finally turn left for a block to our home. Never did I hear either of my parents complain about walking home after working so many hours at the magazi.

Evangelia sewing at the magazi, 1962.

Working At The Magazi

How many times in our lives, did my sister Olympia, my brothers Platon and Johnny, and I, hear the word, magazi? That word kept us, sustained us, nurtured our family since the early 1920's, and most importantly, since the middle 1930's to the present time, through three generations.

As each of the children, Olympia, Platon, Johnny and I reached the age of twelve, we took our turn working at the cleaners. For the children, individually, the magazi was a duty we had to perform. As time went on, each child was given more responsibility and more effort was expected of us.

Johnny wisely observed that many benefits accrued from the work at the magazi. We gained an understanding of the meaning of family. Family. The family grew together, and each of us understood the importance of family. Love and respect for each other in the family brought positive results in a crisis. We knew that in working together as a unit, every member of the family benefitted. The family was all important, not the individual whim or selfish desire of one member. Everyone shared and worked toward a common goal: one goal; the good of all. Unity of purpose was most important for the future well being of everyone. Life was a team effort. The preservation and common welfare of the family was the collective goal, an enduring quality of love and commitment.

For my sister and for me, the first thing we learned to do at the magazi was to mark the clothes for cleaning. Later on, an employee, Troy McCall, taught us how to press the different articles of clothes.

We also assisted our mother with minor sewing. I recall many an hour sitting by my mother's side as she worked at the sewing machine. She taught me how to sew the missing buttons on the clothes, and how to do simple straight hand stitching by sewing cuffs on pants. On occasion she would say to me, in an affectionate way, "kai to katourlio tou botikou, kalo einai kai afto" ("even the urine of the mouse is useful too").

For my brothers, their tasks were a little different. They too did the marking and pressing of clothes, but they also had to learn how to clean hats and block them. Later on, when we got our own dry cleaning machinery, they also had to learn how to spot and clean the clothes as well.

Johnny has remarked that when the boiler shut down, no effort was spared to get it working again with the satisfaction of knowing you did a good job and the cleaners was now productive. Or, the frustration of ruining someone' s clothes and having to deal with a dissatisfied customer. "I understood my importance to the operation of the magazi and why I had to hop the bus from school and go to the magazi. We worked until quitting time and then went home to do homework."

I don' t ever recall complaining or hearing any of my siblings complain about going to work at the cleaners. It was a given. It was as natural as eating, sleeping, a normal function. When our parents told one of us we were expected to go to the magazi to work, we did not whine or complain. We went. Perhaps it was the unspoken feeling that we were a unit as a family, and we all worked for the common good. Or perhaps it was seeing our parents working and struggling so hard to earn a living for us that touched us. Or perhaps it was the refined, matter-of-fact manner in which they told us. Many afternoons after school, if told, one of us would go to the cleaners and work until closing time, nine o' clock.

If we had homework, it was to be done after 9:30 in the evening, when we got home. No one ever said, "I've got homework to do, I can't go to the cleaners". We went, and after we got home, it was up to us to do our homework. I recall also, when I was a teenager, that I wanted to go out on Sunday afternoon with friends. My father would tell my mother, "Why does she want to go out? She should stay home and go to sleep!"

It was my sister Olympia who particularly shouldered the responsibility of taking care of all four of us when my mother first began to work in 1934 at the cleaners. While my mother was gone working, my sister Olympia was in charge at the house. Food was no problem, dinner had already been prepared by my mother earlier in the day. Looking back now, I can see that Olympia had her hands full with my brothers and me. But she managed us all well. I don't ever recall that she complained about supervising us. When she and I were in high school and we wanted to stay for after school activities, the Service Club that Miss Forbes had, Olympia had to hurry home to baby sit our brothers. She did it willingly, with no whining.

For my part, I also went to the magazi willingly. My parents asked me, I did it. My only real problem was years later, after my high school years and beyond. I recall that if I had to go to the cleaners and open up in the morning with my father, I couldn' t wake up. I was a heavy sleeper. My poor father would call me and try to awaken me but many times I wouldn't budge. He would become frustrated, but never cursed, or vented his frustration in any way.

The magazi gave all of us an education. True we all worked all the years that we attended school; but the magazi was there, available, a facility at our disposal, and because of the unselfishness and generosity of our parents, it would see us through our education. Not one of us left school because we had to get a job to support our family. As far as I know, Olympia, Platon and Johnny' s feelings about working at the cleaners were the same as mine.

I worked at the magazi all through school, and after, until I got married. Olympia did too, as did Platon and Johnny. Later on, in the 60's and 70's, Olympia' s son Stefan worked at the magazi, as did my son Elias and my daughter Evangeline; and a few years later, Platon' s two sons, Stephan and Christopher.

Troy McCall

In late 1936 or early 1937 my father employed a black man, Troy McCall, who was originally from the South, the state of Mississippi. He must have been in his late twenties or his thirties. Troy was with us for many years. Johnny recalls that Troy was the first black person he was close to and befriended. He doesn't remember how old he was when he met him, he states he just doesn't remember not knowing Troy. Pressing clothes, cleaning and blocking hats, and shining shoes, Troy did it all.

Johnny recalls that my father preferred to do all the maintenance work and odd jobs that came up at the cleaners, himself. He would on occasion hire others to do them but if he could do the work, he preferred to do it. One day my father told Johnny that a boiler connection was leaking and Troy made a comment about the leak. My father dismissed the comment with the intent of repairing it himself soon. He left the store one day for a short time. When he returned, Troy had fixed the leak. Afterwards my father would mention items that needed attention and Troy would fix them. Johnny feels Troy was eventually involved in everything.

Advertising The Cleaners

I recall hearing my mother tell my father that we would have to do some type of advertising in the neighborhood to let people know of the cleaners. One of the most common forms of advertising at that time were handbills and my parents decided to use that method. One of the points stressed on the fliers as an incentive to lure the customer to the magazi was that missing buttons on the clothes would be replaced free of charge.

Where would they find youngsters to distribute the fliers to the homes on the streets near the magazi on Aldine Avenue, Cote Brillante Avenue, Evans Avenue, Page Boulevard, Taylor Avenue? The elected youngsters, at the beginning, were Olympia and me, ages 13 and 10. Later on, both Platon and Johnny were recruited to pass out the handbills as well. The Cumbarelis girls, Penelope and Julie, also helped with some of the work. We in turn, did the same for their father' s cleaners, in their neighborhood around Delmar Avenue and Sarah Boulevard.

We usually did the delivering of leaflets after school, in the late afternoon. I remember going up and down steps of the homes, occasionally even in the dark. I didn't mind distributing the leaflets. Sometimes it was fun because we did it in pairs, two of us together, never alone. But I do recall thinking as I was distributing the handbills that I was glad the cleaners was not near my school, Washington School on Euclid Avenue. I did not want any of my school friends to see me going up and down steps of the different houses, placing circulars in the mailboxes or under the front door.

The handbills were a successful enterprise, because business did pick up. My mother had a lot of alterations to do, and the free sewing of buttons added to her large pile of work. At different times, both Olympia and I were recruited to sew the missing buttons on the clothes.

Jennie in 1938 with "Henry," the family Ford.

Rewards From The Magazi

For the family, the magazi saw us through the Depression with dignity and sustenance. The magazi taught us hard work was rewarding.

By the end of the decade, the Depression had ended and business at the cleaners picked up. The magazi afforded us luxuries.

We now had telephones at home and at the cleaners.

For the pleasure of their children my parents were able to buy a radio console. It was made of high quality wood with a beautiful mahogany finish. Not just a table radio model, it stood on six legs. It had doors in the front which when opened, exposed the knobs to turn on the radio.

Among the Greek families on Aubert Avenue, we were the first to buy an electric refrigerator, a Norge. Because of its large size, it didn' t quite fit in the kitchen. My mother had the idea of having a section cut in the wall, in the hallway by the kitchen, to accommodate the refrigerator.

My parents even did a little remodeling in the house. They eliminated the sliding wooden doors between the dining room and living room, and had an archway put in.

My father also purchased an automobile (though he never cared about driving it). Even though the Depression continued into the late Thirties, around 1937 the magazi was doing so well that we were able to buy a used car, which made us the second Greek family on Aubert to own an automobile.

Johnny and Platon say the car was a Pontiac. It had four doors. Neither of my parents knew how to drive a car. However, Troy McCall did. He had been a chauffeur in the South before coming to St. Louis. So Troy ended up driving our car, picking up my father in the morning and taking him to work, and bringing him home again in the evening. Then Troy would take the car to his home overnight. Johnny remembers that during the week, Troy would chauffeur individual members of the family. But on Sundays, Troy would drive the Pontiac with the whole family to different places. Troy taught my father how to drive, although I always thought my father was not comfortable behind the wheel. My sister and I, and eventually my mother, learned to drive.

Down the street from the cleaners was the Joe Simpkins Automobile Agency which sold used cars. In the spring of 1938, they had a 1937 Ford that had been repossessed and was selling at a reduced price. Johnny remembers going to the car dealer with our mother. He said she pointed to the car and told him, "This is the car we are getting." He recalls Ford had made a radical change in the design of their cars in 1937, and "I thought it was a 'dumb' looking car. I kept my mouth shut knowing it would do no good to give my opinion." The Pontiac was traded in and we took possession of the new car, our new 1937 two door Ford, blue in color that "went like a jack rabbit", Johnny recalls.

Olympia then was seventeen years old, just a few months shy of eighteen. Troy taught her how to drive, and for all intents and purposes, she became the official family driver. I don't recall my father ever drove after Olympia took over the wheel. Then when I turned sixteen years of age, Olympia and Troy taught me how to drive, and I shared driving responsibilities with my sister for the family.

As the magazi prospered in the late Thirties, my mother bought a set of gold jewelry, a necklace with matching earrings. One day she took me and we went to a jewelry store on Delmar Boulevard, past Euclid Avenue and next to the West End Theater, and looked at the jewelry. She placed a deposit on it, and a week later we went back again to the jewelry store and she paid the balance on it. I don't believe my father ever saw the jewelry before she brought it home. This was the only expensive jewelry that she ever bought for herself that I know of. She gave them to me soon after my father died. I in turn gave them to her namesake, my daughter.

The Reach of The Magazi

In later years the lives of other relatives were touched by the magazi as cousins, aunts, grandchildren and even friends worked there. Their well being was dependent on the prosperity of the magazi.

For a short period, our cousin Dessie worked at the magazi. When she left, my parents hired Katherine Petrides, the daughter of a friend. Even Mary, Harry and Denise Panayotopoulos, Thea Marianthe' s grandchildren, her daughter Io' s children, did not escape their stint at the magazi. They had come to St. Louis in the middle Fifties from Greece. They lived with my mother for a few years, and when they were able, they too worked at the magazi.

To help with the sewing, my mother had Thea Cornelia, the wife of my father' s brother George, helping her. She worked there for several years, and later, Despina Lazanas assisted my mother. When Thea Marianthe came from Greece on several visits, she helped my mother out during particularly busy periods, with the alterations at the magazi. When World War II was over, the magazi also nurtured and supported our destitute and displaced relatives in Greece. Not only was money sent generously to relatives to rebuild their disrupted lives, but other help as well.

We were fortunate that the cleaners had accumulated unclaimed clothes that had been cleaned and pressed, hanging in their paper bags. Countless boxes were filled with those clothes (including many of our personal clothes), packaged and mailed to Greece to relatives on both sides of the family, my father' s and mother's. My mother even sent clothing to destitute people she did not know, people who had gotten our address and written to my mother asking for help.

Thea Marianthe had also written and requested a welding machine for her son Niko so he could restart his business devastated by the war. Fortunately, through our financial help and that of various members of the family, a welding machine was found, bought, packaged, and shipped to Greece. This kindness was never forgotten by Niko and years later when we went to Greece on a trip, Niko insisted on giving me money to buy gold jewelry for my sister Olympia and for myself.

Even before that generous gesture, grateful relatives from Greece sent us beautiful handmade silk blouses, Greek plates, and vases. They never forgot our help to them in their hour of need, and reciprocated our kindness. Even in 1965 on our first family trip to Greece, Niko' s son Foti, gave us the use of his newly built apartment to stay in. We stayed there for two months.

A year after the first welding machine was sent to Niko, a second one was also shipped to Greece. Through the generous financial contribution of the same family members, it went to Thea Marianthe's younger son Kosta.

Moving

Eventually, the cleaners was moved to 4510 Easton Avenue. Platon and I believe it was the summer of 1946 when we bought the 4510 building in the next block and moved from 4480. Platon says when we moved, the shoe shining part had been done away with. Some of the old chairs had been originally stored in the basement of the house on Aubert Avenue.

Alterations and modifications were done to the existing building, machines for cleaning clothes were put in, and to accommodate them the building was extended in the back. The building was bought originally for $19,000 to $20,000. The addition added in the back of the building cost about $15,000 to $20,000. Concrete was laid approximately for 80 feet. The building is about 100 feet from front to back, and about 30 feet wide. A boiler room was added. The third floor was completely torn off, plus a section of the second floor which was the back porch.

With the expansion of the building, we were able to do wholesale cleaning of clothes and hats, 200 to 300 hats a week! One of our customers was the White Line Laundry. We did very well until some of our competition started to undercut our prices on the clothes and hats.

The cleaners is in a designated historic area of St. Louis. The Visitation Catholic Church located in the back of the cleaners on Taylor Avenue, became a historic landmark. This area encompassed the cleaners so the cleaners is now technically in the historic area. The area includes the south side of Martin Luther King Drive, to the north side of Page Avenue and all of Evans Avenue, beginning from the west side of Sarah Avenue to 80 feet west of the store, which also is the end of the church yard.

Uncle George and father Stefan with Jennie, 1926.

Character

One of the proudest moments for me, in my association with my father was when he had become an American citizen in 1941. I drove him to the polling place to vote for his first time. Missouri was voting for a Senator to Congress. A newcomer, Harry Truman, was the Democratic candidate. My father voted for Truman, and he explained to me, "The Democrats are for the working man. The Republicans are for the rich people." I have never forgotten his words.

In our home there was no bitchiness or complaining on the part of either parent. My mother often said that bitchiness brought evil (grousouzia) into the home, and the fortunes of the family suffered.

My mother was also a refined person, not vulgar, a kind and generous person, compassionate. After World War II she helped many unfortunate relatives and friends in Greece. Her method of discipline to me was to say, "A good girl does not act like that. Don' t let it happen again." She never struck any of her children.

My parents had good habits and standards that their children follow today. They had the spiritual gift of administering correction to their children with gentleness.

After my mother reconciled herself to the fact that the United States was to be her permanent home, she made an effort to learn the English language. I have a copy of a Certificate of Award, stating: *Angela Constantinides, during the year 1925–1926, has been faithful in her attendance upon the English class conducted by the Board of Religious Organizations of Saint Louis, Missouri and has been present at the number of sessions required for the attainment of the certificate. Awarded on this twelfth day of June 1926. Signed, Mrs. Clara W. Hopper, Teacher; and Irene T. Kuhn, Director of Americanization, Board of Religious Organizations.*

This activity occurred at the time my mother had two young children, my sister and me. I was just two years old.

She made another attempt at learning English, in the early Thirties before the Depression made its forceful impact. At that time, she attended English classes at Washington Elementary School on Euclid Avenue. They were held after the regular school day, and Platon remembers going with her to the school and waiting for her.

In spite of these attempts to learn English, my mother very rarely spoke the language. I feel she was conscious of her limited knowledge, and perhaps she felt that she didn't really need to express herself in English.

My mother was very proud of the fact that she became an American citizen. I recall the time she was studying the information given to her concerning the examination. We all tried to coach her, giving her a little history of the different presidents and other background information. In exasperation, one day she informed us that if the judge denied her American citizenship, she would tell him "If you want to make me an American citizen, all right. If you don't, I am a good woman. I have four good children. I am a good person".

Needless to say, that explanation to the judge was unnecessary; my mother passed her citizenship examination without any problem, and with much pride, became an American citizen. She regularly voted in political elections, a Democrat.

Olympia and Jennie, 1927.

Platon's Wintry Birth

January 4, 1930 was the day my brother Platon was born. I recall the day vividly. I was five and a half years old. The doctor was a female doctor, Dr. Rose Minnie Rose, one of the few women doctors in that period of time. She had been called to come to our house because my mother was ready to give birth. Dr. Rose was patronized by the Greeks on our street, and had delivered many of the Greek children on Aubert Avenue, including my sister Olympia and me, and later would deliver my brother Johnny too. Many years later, Dr. Rose was still practicing medicine and she would attend to the birth of my nephew Stefan and the births of my children Evangeline and Elias.

I don't know how Dr. Rose had been contacted when my mother was ready to give birth to my brother Platon because we had no telephone or automobile. We lived at 761 Aubert Avenue, and Dr. Rose's office was at least a mile away, at the corner of Union and Easton Avenues. Her office was on the second floor, above a store.

It was in the middle of winter, a bitterly cold day. The streets, sidewalks, trees, everything was covered with ice. My mother was in the back bedroom which had a fireplace. There was wood on the grate, burning. The room was warm and cozy.

My father, sister Olympia and I were anxiously awaiting the arrival of the doctor. I went to the living room. I was too short to reach the window, so I dragged a chair to the window and climbed up. I could now easily look out the large window, up and down the street. Nothing stirred on the street, no cars, no people, no animals. Soon an old black Model T Ford, a Tin Lizzie as they were called at the time, came slowly rolling down the street on thin spindly tires and stopped in front of our house. There were no other cars parked on the street.

A small, slim woman, all bundled up from head to toe, wearing a long black coat reaching to the ground and a black hat covering her ears and all her hair, got out of the car on the passenger side. She reached into the front seat of the car and pulled out a medical bag. Dr. Rose had arrived.

I watched her as she slowly, carefully and laboriously held on to the metal banister and climbed the ice covered steps from the sidewalk below to the terrace above, about ten to twelve steps. The sidewalk on the terrace to the front porch

51

steps was also ice-covered. I saw her hold onto the banister with one hand and, with the other hand, hold onto her medical bag. She held the bag high above the sidewalk, and twisted her arm like a pitcher ready to throw a baseball. She gave the bag a strong swing and threw it on the ground toward the porch steps.

The medical bag slid on the ice, and came to rest at the bottom of the porch steps. A perfect landing. Dr. Rose then carefully held on to the fence as she walked to the porch steps. Then she picked up her medical bag with one hand, and with the other hand holding onto the wooden railing, she came up the final steps to the porch. She had successfully maneuvered the treacherous ice-covered path.

When she reached the porch, my father went and welcomed her into the house. Platon was born shortly after.

Housework

On Saturdays, my mother would leave early in the morning with my father, and she would tell Olympia and me what chores we had to do in the house. Cleaning the house topped the list. Every week there was the bathroom to be cleaned. The linoleum of the long hallway that stretched the length of the house, to be mopped from the front door to the kitchen. Plus the mopping of the kitchen linoleum floor. Dusting furniture in the living and dining rooms was also on our schedule.

I would write my chores down on paper. Needless to say, I never completed all the jobs I had to do. When my mother came home in the evening and saw that I had not accomplished all she had asked me to do, she did not raise her voice, or become irritated with me. All she would say to me was, "Monon pou ta egrapses kato." (It was enough for you to write them down.)

I recall Olympia and I doing the laundry. First, we would have to light the gas heater for hot water so the water would be the right temperature for washing the clothes. My mother had a washing machine. In those days the machines were very different from the kind we have now. It consisted of a tumbler, a round drum where the clothes would be put in. The tumbling action would wash the clothes. We would have to take the clothes carefully out of the hot water while they were in the tumbler, by hand, then put them through the wringer into the rinsing tub. Then by hand again pass them through the wringer to have the rinse water squeezed out. Now the clothes were ready to be hung up to dry.

If the weather was nice, we would hang the clothes to dry on the clothesline we had strung up in the back yard. We had a big wicker basket, with a handle at each end. Olympia and I unloaded the clothes from the washing machine, placed them in the basket. We each grabbed a handle and carried the basket up the three steps from the basement to the backyard. Then we hung the clothes on the clothesline. To keep the middle of the clothesline from sagging, with the risk of having the clothes drag on the ground, we had a long pole with a v notched in one end. We would slip the v under the clothesline, and raise it several feet off the ground. If it was winter, or the weather was bad, there were lines already strung in the basement for us to hang the clothes.

My mother never imposed on the neighbor upstairs, Mrs. Laskaris, or on my uncle Demo or his wife, aunt Anna, or the next door Greek neighbors, to keep a watchful eye over us. I guess she felt Olympia could handle three younger siblings, although Olympia herself was only thirteen years old when my mother started working at the magazi.

The high school graduate in front of 761 Aubert, 1941.

Greek School

As an adult, one day when I was teaching at Baden Public School, in St. Louis, one of the teachers and I were discussing an after school math program. My mind drifted back fifty years to the days when as a child I also attended an after school program. It was Greek school; a private program not sponsored by Federal funds.

As a child living on Aubert Avenue, my family was one of fourteen Greek families situated in a two block area. The parents were all from Greece and Asia Minor. They had resided fifteen to twenty years in this country.

The Greek fathers spoke some English, mostly broken and only one father, mine, had had a college education in the old country. One of the languages he had learned was English. He had a good vocabulary in the language and could communicate quite well.

The Greek mothers, with no exception, knew very little or almost no English at all. They conversed totally in Greek.

These Greek immigrants wanted one very important thing for their children. They all wanted their children to learn to read and write Greek. Speaking Greek for the children was no problem; that was the principal language in the home. The children spoke English outside the home while playing with friends, or at school, but at home, the Greek language was the only spoken communication among the members of the family.

To teach the children to read and write Greek was of prime importance. Some parents who had a little education could teach their children, but they did not have the time, the materials, and in many cases, the patience.

Fortunately there was a qualified individual of Greek nationality in the community who was also a fairly recent immigrant to St. Louis from her native Constantinople in Asia Minor. Her name was Efthemia Andreadou.

Kyria Efthemia was born to be a teacher. Kyria Efthemia had impeccable credentials. She had a good reputation. She had also had formal training as a teacher in her native city.

She came to St. Louis in the early Twenties, and a marriage was arranged with a compatriot. He was a truck driver for a Greek owned bakery. He wore glasses and was a happy man, smiling all the time, in contrast to her austere, glaring countenance. She wore glasses, which gave greater emphasis to the stern look constantly present on her face. They were childless.

She was strict in every sense of the word. Not only in the discipline of her classroom, where Kyria Efthemia demanded and got the undivided attention of her pupils. She was also able to motivate her charges and they responded to her with lessons well prepared and well learned. That, in spite of the fact none of the students were thrilled at the prospect of giving up three afternoons a week to go to her class after the regular public school had been dismissed.

All of Kyria Efthemia's pupils walked to Greek School, some as much as a mile, in heat and cold (no one rode in an automobile, because no parent owned a car). To ride the street car to attend the Greek School was out of the question. The fare for a child under twelve was a nickel one way, ten cents for those above the age of twelve. Round trip fare of ten cents or twenty cents to spend for one child was too much money in the financially troubled times of the Depression. Occasionally, if it rained, my parents did give money to my sister and to me to go to Greek School by street car, but as a rule, we walked as did everyone else.

The school was located in a rented store. In the years of the early Thirties, it was called just plain, unadorned Greek School. Now it is referred to as Greek Cultural School, not quite as harsh a term. Plain Greek School might give the impression of a sore thumb sticking out, but Greek Cultural School has the feel of presenting a softer image, blending in more with the American way of life.

The students who attended Kyria Efthemia's classes came from several areas near Taylor and Finney Avenues, About ten children from our street, Aubert Avenue, made up our group. Our group consisted of older sisters and brothers from the upper grades, who waited impatiently for younger sisters and brothers from the lower grades to meet in front of the school building. We did not go home first, instead we started off on our walk to Greek School.

Our small group formed as we met outside of the Washington Elementary School building on Euclid Avenue when school was dismissed for the day. Washington Elementary School had been built in1893 of red brick. It was a severe, plain-looking building, with no fancy exterior adornments such as towers or spires that some of the other public school edifices had. The building itself gave the impression that no nonsense would be tolerated there. There were three floors, about ten classrooms. A nurse and a doctor came weekly to the school.

Our itinerary to Greek School began from Washington School, south on Euclid Avenue to the corner. Turn left, going east at Fountain Avenue, bordering Fountain Park.

The park was oval in shape and stretched for three blocks. In the center of the park was an ornate, sculptured fountain, reminiscent of fountains found in Rome. Water cascaded down the sides and splashed into the basin. I recall that many times as youngsters, my siblings and I, on a hot humid St. Louis summer day, would lean over the side of the fountain and let the water splash on us, cooling us. We would giggle and scream with delight as we cooled off.

Fountain Avenue had large beautiful two and three story brick homes facing the park, with well-trimmed yards. We continued east two blocks, past Bayard Avenue and Walton Avenue, to Lewis Place which was a private street. The entrance to Lewis Place had an inspiring Arch built by the original developer of the area. It was quite impressive and an inspiration to the young students in search of their mother language. Lewis Place was lit by gas lights and was two blocks long. It had a center parkway lined on both sides with dignified homes that had been built between 1890 and 1928. Lewis Place is now a part of the National Register Historic District.

I was always very impressed as we walked through Lewis Place because there was a Greek family living there, the Nanos family. Phillip, the son, also attended our Greek school. The father had made his money in the theater business, owning several. It was a well-known fact that he had sent a lot of money to the old country to his village in Epirus, Greece to build a school, and he gave money for other causes as well. One day on our way to Greek school, I saw an African American woman in a maid's uniform sweeping their front porch. It was an impressive scene that I have never forgotten.

Another majestic arch designated the end of Lewis Place, coming out at Taylor Avenue. Our group then turned left going north, immediately facing a row of four stores next to our final destination.

There were no snacks awaiting us at Greek school, nor did anyone have any spending money to stop on our way at a confectionary or a grocery store to buy anything. Fortunately, there was a candy store next to the store Kyria Efthemia had rented for our classes. On the rare occasion one of us would have a penny to spend, we would stop in at the candy store.

For a penny one could buy several pieces of licorice, hard candy, etc. If one wasn't able to eat all the candy before class started, they would try and sneak and put some in their mouth when they thought Kyria Efthimia wasn't looking. That was not the wisest thing to do; invariably they were caught and chastised for their behavior.

Greek school was Kyria Efthemia's own undertaking. The parents paid her directly for her services. The store she had rented for our classes was plain. There was no covering on the store windows, and I imagine a passerby could look in and see the classes in session. On the walls she had hung pictures of the heroes of the Greek War of Independence: Kolocotronis, Athanasios Diakos, Karaiskakis, Papaflessas. Dark-haired, grim-looking, mustachioed faces staring down at us as we tried to learn the language of our parents.

There was a portable blackboard, a teacher's desk, and five rows of student's desks, about five in each row to accommodate the twenty-one or twenty-two students. Kyria Efthemia taught all six grades, all levels, her students ranging in age from seven to fourteen years.

In her classroom was an ever present stick placed within close range, to use freely at her discretion, rightly or wrongly. She was a stern taskmaster, who thought nothing of hitting the children, girls or boys, with her stick. Even I was not excluded from that policy. It was true that some of the older boys, the Thavorides boys, Jimmy, George and Tony, Philip Nanos, and others were restless and playful, but never to the point where it was necessary to be struck with the stick. In general, the students were well behaved and quiet during class time. At almost every class, one of the older boys would manage to break her stick or leave with it when she was not aware of it. At the next class, undaunted by the event of the previous class, she would bring a new stick to the classroom.

Kyria Efthemia did not provide hooks for us for our coats, so when the weather turned cold, we had to keep our wraps at our desks. Sometimes that could be a problem, because the more articles of clothing we had, the more cumbersome and restricted our seats were. On one occasion, when I should have been studying my Greek lesson, and I thought Kyria Efthemia was preoccupied with one of the older groups, I got up out of my seat to straighten my coat which had gotten rumpled up to arrange it better on my seat. Out of nowhere, I heard the whoosh of an object, and felt a long, thin object across my back, accompanied by a sharp pain. Kyria Efthemia had come around in back of me while I was standing up and arranging my things, and whacked me across my back!

It stunned me, and hurt quite a bit.

When I went home, and for a week afterward, I complained my back hurt. My mother would rub it with ointment. The only problem was, my point of emphasis shifted, and I would point to different parts of my back and say the pain was coming from there. My mother was mystified by the shifting of the pain. My parents never complained, or said a word to Kyria Efthemia about her hitting me on the back with the stick. Instead, my mother admonished me, and told me that next time I should be more careful when I arranged my wraps. I should not disturb the teacher.

As it was, I was one of the youngest in the class. My parents felt it expedient to send me to Greek school because my sister Olympia, who was three years my senior, was enrolled in the fourth grade class. Olympia was quiet, obedient and a model student. Kyria Efthemia never had an occasion to correct her, verbally or otherwise, in any way.

There was only one other child close to my age at Greek school, our next door neighbor, Alex John. She was almost a year older than I was. Our family and hers were koumbari, my mother had baptized her brother Pete. Alex and I were very good friends, both socially oriented, very talkative. We sat one in back of the other and were constantly reprimanded for our talking to each other.

One of my fondest memories of going to and coming home from Greek school was the camaraderie of the group. I felt, even though I was one of the youngest, that I was accepted by the older children, particularly the girls. I was equal to them. Friends such as Bessie Laskaris, and Lillian Marsellos were the leaders of the group, the trend setters among the girls. They knew many of the latest popular songs, and would sing them with fervor and happiness. Songs such as Winter Wonderland and Walking My Baby Back Home were favorites of theirs. We all learned the songs from them.

The boys in the group were also friendly, but full of mischief. Pete John, Nicky Marsellos, Nick Laskaris. Their biggest joy was to tease the girls, to chase them, to try and take their belongings from them and toss them back and forth to each other. The boys were particularly annoying to the girls in winter, when it got dark early. Their biggest scheme was to frighten the girls, to run ahead and hide behind a car or bush, throw pebbles or rocks as the girls approached, or jump out of their hiding places and scare the girls. The girls would yell, or run away, or fuss at the boys, but secretly I think they enjoyed it. No parent ever confronted another parent about the boys' behavior. The parents felt that it was natural for children to act in those ways. The parents were happy to have the children go to and come home from Greek school in a group, they felt their children were safer that way.

I sometimes think of the little group from Washington Elementary School, the days of trudging and plodding to and from Greek School. There was a spirit of friendly goodwill among the children, a gregariousness, good fellowship, sociability, cheer. For me, I felt I was accepted by my peers, even though they were older. I looked up to them as role models, and I was a part of them. I don't recall anyone of the group being mean, or critical, or speaking harshly to me. They liked me, and accepted me as I was. Being in their company, I felt a part of them. It helped me develop self-confidence, self-esteem. I never expressed any thoughts that were negative about Greek School, in spite of Kyria Efthemia's difficult ways. I went willingly. I was happy to go.

The closeness our little group developed during those years stayed with all of us through the rest of our years of education, and even after everyone was married. We had established an unspoken bond, a friendship that continues to this day.

The Demos Glitsos wedding, 1926. Jennie is in the center, held by the Uncle Demos.

Quarantine

Our family always lived on the first floor of our two family flat. I remember my parents had usually rented the flat upstairs to roomers, individual boarders, not the whole unit to a single family.

In 1932, my parents decided to rent the first floor to my Uncle Demos, Aunt Anna, and their three daughters. My parents, my older sister Olympia, my two younger brothers Platon and Johnny and I moved upstairs. In 1934, my sister Olympia was thirteen years old, and I was ten years old. We were in elementary school. My brother Platon, who was born in 1930, was four years old, a preschooler. My youngest brother John was just a toddler.

Platon got sick one day. My parents thought it was a minor, childhood illness; fever, sore throat, restlessness. My mother tried to treat it with her standard remedies. Aspirin for the fever. Common home treatment for sore throats at the time was the liberal use of Vicks Vaporub. She would rub the Vicks, which had its own distinctive pungent smell on the throat, then cover it with a handkerchief. (Even more than sixty years later the smell of Vicks Vaporub evokes childhood memories.) However, no home treatment seemed to make Platon feel better.

Though St. Louis did not have a large Greek community, an enclave of fifteen Greek families lived in the two-block area of Aubert Avenue. All our Greek neighbors suggested their own remedies, but none were effective in treating my little brother. None of them seemed to make him feel better.

When Platon's fever continued to rise my parents took the extreme step of having a doctor, Dr. Kohler, come to the house. He was a man in his fifties. He was known to the family and was a neighbor who lived across the street. The only other time I ever recall a doctor at our home was when my mother gave birth to my younger brothers.

He examined Platon, and prescribed medicine. Platon did not get better, as a matter of fact, he seemed to be getting worse. He had a high fever, and had difficulty breathing. Dr. Kohler said in a second visit to our home a few days later that in his professional opinion, Platon had to be immediately hospitalized since he had diphtheria, a serious contagious disease which at the time struck terror in the hearts of all parents. Platon could not under any circumstances remain in the house any longer. He had to go to the hospital at once. In the 1930's diphtheria was a dreaded disease.

My father, whose Anatolian upbringing had made him reserved, lost all control of his emotions. While he didn't have the money to pay for the hospital, my father said to the doctor, "I will sell everything that I own, even my shoes, if I have to," my father promised, "as long as Platon gets proper medical care."

That's why perhaps, even though it has been over sixty years, I clearly remember my father's impassioned pleas to the doctor. The hospital! It was unthinkable. The hospital brought to mind the worst possible thoughts. How many people survived going to the hospital? In our minds, the hospital was the last stop before the funeral parlor.

My father had named his first born son after his own brother, Platon, who had died in 1928. My father's brother had survived the Catastrophe and left Smyrna as a refugee. He had become an important surgeon in the Greek Army. He had been vaccinated to travel to Paris, where he was to study the latest surgical techniques, but one of the needles that had been used was dirty and he got blood poisoning and died in a few days. He was only thirty years old.

Now my father was wondering whether his own son would live. Platon was taken to City Hospital, the only one of two public hospitals that would accept a patient with a highly contagious disease. In segregated St. Louis, City Hospital was for white people and Homer G. Phillips Hospital for black people.

I don't remember how or who took Platon to City Hospital. It was located quite a distance from our house, on the extreme southern edge of downtown St. Louis. We had no car, nor did any of our Greek friends, nor any of the other neighbors.

Though only thirteen years old, Olympia, as the eldest child, was entrusted with the care of our youngest brother Johnny, then two years old. I was the designated escort for my mother's daily trips to the hospital, with the task to maneuver the city's transportation even though I was only ten years old. Visiting Platon at the hospital became a daily ordeal. The forty-five minute trip would involve three streetcars. My mother and I would board the Delmar streetcar at the Aubert Avenue stop going east, ride and transfer to the Broadway streetcar and go south, transfer to the Jefferson line until we reached City Hospital.

I was an extremely verbal child and was charged with being my mother's translator when necessary, with streetcar conductors, doctors and hospital administrators. My father's day ruled out any hospital visits. He opened the store at eight o'clock in the morning, and closed at nine in the evening. Home by ten o'clock, just in time to eat dinner and go to bed. Up again at six o'clock in the morning to get ready to go to work.

As if the forty-five minute trip to the hospital by streetcar was not enough, during our first visit we were asked, if we could afford to bring oranges for the patients. Since we were not being charged for Platon's hospital stay, from that day on, my mother and I carried several large bags of oranges as we transferred from one streetcar line to the next to comply with the hospital request, the gift of oranges.

Our daily trips to the hospital were hardly reassuring. Since Platon was in isolation we were never allowed into his room. Instead my mother and I would stand outside his first floor window and wave. Good days were ones when we got a wave and a smile back.

My mother, whether from her background in Smyrna as a Greek living under Turkish domination or from the pain of being an immigrant whose home in Asia Minor had disappeared, had learned to keep her vulnerabilities to herself. During the long trips on the streetcars and during the time of looking at her first born son through a hospital window, she was quiet and subdued. She was possibly thinking, what would the outcome be?

Soon after Platon was admitted to the hospital we faced new difficulties. An official from the Health Department came and posted a large red sign on the front door which said the house was quarantined and everyone was officially prohibited from entering the premises. Luckily, relatives and close Greek friends, including several from Asia Minor, ignored the Health Department order, proving that regional and ethnic ties were stronger than the drive to fully adapt to the laws of their new land. Not to blatantly disregard the quarantine order, they used a side entrance that was not visible from the street. Olympia and I were also forbidden from attending school or even going out into the yard to play with friends. We, too, were in isolation.

More than a week after Platon had been in the hospital, a policeman arrived at our home on Aubert Avenue and asked to speak to my mother. We had no telephone, the hospital couldn't call us to notify us of any change in my brother's condition. Since the police only came to your home to bring bad news, we were terrified. But he had come to tell us that Platon was getting better and was now well enough to leave the hospital. He did not have diphtheria, after all. Dr. Kohler had misdiagnosed him. He only had had a high fever with heavy congestion. A common childhood illness.

Since Progressive Cleaners also had no phone, my father didn't learn the good news until he came home from work that evening. He was so angry that the doctor had needlessly put us through such distress that he wanted to go across the street to beat Dr. Kohler up. My mother calmed him down and the crises was over.

Until we moved away from Aubert Avenue in 1944, our family never called upon Dr. Kohler for professional assistance again. My sister, brothers and I avoided walking on the other side of the street and passing Dr. Kohler's house. His gross mistake was something we could never forget.

Nikos Kassimatis, 1915.

Venetia And Niko

They were an odd looking couple. He was tall, slim, angular. His face was thin and long. He had a full head of curly, gray hair. She was short and stout, her face was round, and the years had mellowed her features into skin that was soft to the touch. Her hair was gray, curlier than his. When she was working hard, strands of her hair would stick out of her head, like railroad crossing signals. She kept her hair cut short, an odd habit for Greek women of the 1920s and 30s, who usually kept their hair long and in a bun at the back of their necks. When looking at theo Niko and thea Venetia, one got the feeling of a Greek Mutt and Jeff couple.

Although my sister, brothers, and I called them thea Venetia and theo Niko, as if they were our aunt and uncle, they were not close relatives. Theo Niko was a distant relative of my mother's. Yet, our families were very close.

My earliest recollection of them was as a young child in the early Thirties, when they unexpectedly arrived at our home one day. They came from a small coal mining town, West Frankfort, Illinois, about an hour's drive away from St. Louis. About ten years earlier, theo Niko had sold his shoe shine, hat and dry cleaning business at 4966 Delmar Boulevard in St. Louis to move to West Frankfort. This was done on the recommendation of friends, the two Notaras brothers, who lived nearby in another Illinois small town, DuQuion. They told theo Niko of a Greek man in West Frankfort who wanted to sell his hat and dry cleaning business to move back to Greece to live. Intrigued by the thought of an opportunity to purchase a thriving business, he sold the store on Delmar, and he and thea Venetia moved to West Frankfort.

Unfortunately, as the Depression hit, the coal mine in West Frankfort closed. Unable to keep the business, they drove back to St. Louis in their old black Model T Ford crammed full of all their belongings. My parents had no indication they were coming to St. Louis and they appeared at our home with no place to stay. There was no one else who could take them in. My parents felt sorry for them, and agreed to allow them to stay in our home until they got on their feet.

Our family was living on Aubert Avenue then. The Depression as yet had not affected my father's business. Financially, our family was in good condition. Our home had two bedrooms. The one Olympia and I had, and the other one my parents had. My parents gave theo Niko and thea Venetia our bedroom. It had a double bed in it. My mother put another double bed in the dining room, and Olympia and I slept there. My brothers slept on the daybed in my parent's bedroom.

Theo Niko and thea Venetia stayed with our family six months. In all that time and for all the years we knew theo Niko, no matter what his financial situation, he always managed to have a car. He did not want to work for anyone else. The Greek desire of having his own business prevailed, and he looked around for a store to start his own cleaners again. After several months theo Niko was able to rent a small store on Union Avenue, put in a pressing machine, a few blocks for hats, and he was in business.

Thea Venetia was able to get a job through a Greek friend, Annie Marcellos, a patriotisa, who lived across the street from us on Aubert Avenue, and who worked in a laundry owned by a Greek man. Thea Venetia's job was to iron laundry, and she did that work standing on her feet all day long. She kept that job for about a year, until her husband's new venture began to show some success. She left the laundry, and worked in the cleaners with him as a seamstress.

Theo Niko had been born and raised in Smyrna. He had come to the United States in the early 1900's, under what circumstances I never knew. I wonder, perhaps, when the Turkish government passed a law in 1910 stating that all Greek men were subject to serve in the Turkish army, had this prompted his move to the United States? Many Greek men had immigrated to this country at that time. He had no close relatives in this country. He was all alone. On several occasions he was fond of telling the story that when he was a youngster in Smyrna, he had a job going door to door selling milk. He would furbish the story by telling us how he watered the milk down before setting out on his rounds. He was particularly elated when he told of how the housewives were unaware that he had put one over on them, by selling them the watered down milk.

Thea Venetia had been born on the island of Chios. As a child, she had been sent to Smyrna to work in a wealthy home as a maid, which was a common practice of the time for the children of poor families. She was a very good cook, and she attributed that ability to the fact that she learned her cooking skills from the cooks in the wealthy home where she was a maid. She too had no relatives in the United States. I had never heard her speak of the Catastrophe of Smyrna, I believe she had left Turkey before that holocaust.

She and theo Niko had fallen in love, but it was ten years after he left Smyrna that they were reunited and she was able to come to the United States where they were married.

I always had a soft spot in my heart for thea Venetia because she had no children. She would have made a wonderful mother because she was a loving, kind hearted, warm person. She did not criticize or malign other people. She constantly strove to help her husband in any and every way she could, and to take care of both their needs.

One year for Mother's Day, when I was about 10 or 11 years old, I asked my mother if we could get thea Venetia a gift since she had no children of her own. My mother agreed. My mother had a planter which she didn't want anymore. I thought it was very nice, I liked it. It wasn't very big, about 8 inches long, and 6 inches high. It had the shape of two small elephants, side by side, open at the top, for a plant. My mother and I went to a florist, who put a plant in it. I don't remember what kind of leaf plant we got her, but it looked very good.

By that time, theo Niko and thea Venetia were living in a three room house across the street from us. It was similar to a row house. Upon entering there was a living room, then a bedroom, a kitchen and a bathroom, all in a straight line, from the front to the back of the house.

On Mother's Day we took the plant to her house. She was so pleased, she actually was speechless, saying, "For me? For me? Why? Why?". I don't know if she knew the significance of Mother's Day. She was visibly touched. It made me feel good, just as good as when I gave my mother her Mother's Day gift.

I recently found a diary I had kept when I was thirteen years old and after reading it, I remembered the many times our families shared special occasions. One entry I have is Saturday, January 1, 1938, that I had written, "Last night theo Niko and thea Venetia, with theo Demo, thea Anna and my cousins Joanna, Marie and Dessie, my parents, sister and brothers, welcomed the New Year by playing cards, the game of 31."

In 1938 money was hard to come by, particularly for children, and no matter how small the amount, it had a special meaning. St. John's Feast Day is January 7. In my diary I had written that on January 9, when our family was celebrating the religious holiday, thea Venetia gave me a dime for my nameday. It was an important moment for me, and the significance of it made a lasting impression on me so that I recorded it in my diary. I don't remember what I did with the money. On that day we celebrated my nameday and also Johnny's and Joanna's nameday, besides Platon's birthday, which was January 4. I don't know if thea Venetia rewarded them also.

Even though at the time I was only thirteen years old, I was knowledgeable about the city of St. Louis, and with public transportation, could find my way fairly easily around the city. I was also bilingual, knowing Greek almost as well as the English language. I served as interpreter for my mother frequently. In my diary, I have two notations, one for Thursday March 3 when after school I walked one block south from Blewett High School from Enright Avenue to Delmar Avenue. I boarded the Delmar streetcar going east. I got off at Jefferson and Washington Avenues where theo Niko's cleaners were, and met thea Venetia, to take her downtown to shop for furniture. We boarded the Delmar streetcar at Washington Avenue, going east, and got off at Sixth Street. Thea Venetia did buy something, I don't record in my diary what it was, but I made the comment it was "very pretty."

Thea Venetia must have been pleased with my navigational and interpretative skills, because almost a week later, on Wednesday March 9, I again went to theo Niko's cleaners by streetcar. I followed the same routine, walking from Blewett High School one block south from Enright Avenue to Delmar Avenue, taking the Delmar streetcar going east. Again I got off at Jefferson and Washington Avenues where theo Niko's cleaners were, and met thea Venetia. She and I again boarded the Delmar streetcar at Washington Avenue, going east to downtown, and got off at Sixth street. She bought furniture.

On another occasion, on April 3, my parents had a houseful of visitors: theo Demos' family, George, Tula and Mrs. Alexandres, Mrs. Laskaris, Alex's mother and stepfather Mr. and Mrs. Charbas, Christopher and his mother Mrs. Vlahopoulos, thea Venetia and theo Niko.

When my husband Elia and I started going together, he was staying with the Paspalas', his aunt, uncle and cousins. However, it came time for him to move out of his uncle's home. He asked thea Venetia if she would rent him a room in the flat they were renting on Wells Avenue. There was a small, vacant room at the front of the house she was not using. She agreed, and Elia lived there for about a year until we got married. Thea Venetia liked Elia, and on one occasion she said to him, "Let me adopt you as my son!" Of course, theo Niko was still alive then, and that would have been impossible to do.

Shortly after World War II, theo Niko and thea Venetia bought a piece of property, a city lot on a side street near the Small Arms plant on Goodfellow and Natural Bridge Avenues. They were very proud of it. It was a topic of many conversations they had with friends. They originally bought the lot to build a house on it, but as the years passed by, theo Niko's health deteriorated. He developed diabetes, which in time caused the amputation of both of his legs, each at a different time.

Before his illness, theo Niko spent many Sunday mornings at the lot, planting a vegetable garden, cutting the grass. For them, after all the years of hard work, living in rented houses, the lot was an achievement and an accomplishment. It held the promise of the dream to build a home on it and finally own their own home. But it was not to be.

In 1957 during the early morning hours, a tornado hit the city of St. Louis. By then Elia and I owned our own home on Melvin Avenue. We were fortunate. The tornado had taken a northeast direction through the city, avoiding our area. The telephone lines were still functioning, and I immediately called my family, my mother, my sister Olympia, my brother Platon, to inquire about tornado damage. All were safe. No damage had been done to their homes. I heard on the news the path the tornado had taken was into the area where thea Venetia and theo Niko lived, Grand and Garrison Avenues.

I called thea Venetia and she told me their home had been damaged by the tornado. Windows had been blown out, the wind and rain had damaged the interior, and they wouldn't be able to spend the night there.

Elia and I told her I would go after school that day and bring them to our house to stay until their home was repaired and in livable condition. When I went to pick them up at 4 o'clock I had to pick my way across the sidewalk. A large tree had been uprooted and was in my way. Glass from broken windows was in the back bedroom and in the living room, with water on the furniture and floor. The broken windows had been covered by plywood. The Greek owner of the house who lived upstairs, Kyria Despina, came down, and assured us that help was on the way. She had been notified by the authorities that cleanup crews provided by the Red Cross and city would take care of the damage from the water. She assured us it would be safe to leave the house, and theo Niko and thea Venetia could come with me.

When I first entered the house, theo Niko and thea Venetia were wearing their coats. They were huddled in the kitchen in front of the oven, trying to keep warm. By that time, theo Niko had been forced into retirement by the loss of a leg due to his illness. I helped them gather up a few belongings, and I drove them to our home on Melvin Avenue.

Elia and I gave up our bedroom to theo Niko and thea Venetia. Elia slept in the children's room in one of the twin beds that the children had. Evangeline and Eliake slept in the other twin bed, they were small enough so that the bed accommodated them. I remember sleeping on the living room couch.

We kept them at our home for a week, long enough for their house to be made livable again, repaired and cleaned up. Then we drove them back to their home.

Both theo Niko and thea Venetia were frugal in their habits. Around 1952, theo Niko did indulge himself in buying a new car, green in color, a Plymouth. His only vice was smoking cigarettes. Thea Venetia was even more frugal than her husband, watching that every penny was spent carefully. She spent very little money on herself but did manage to look presentable and neat in public. When they died, they left a bank account of $33,000, which for that period of time, was a good deal of money. She was not even aware of how much money they had.

On St. Nicholas Day, December 6, thea Venetia always celebrated her husband's name day. We always enjoyed going there for his name day because we were impressed with several items she had brought from Smyrna as part of her trousseau.

In her bedroom, on the dresser, she had a beautiful icon of the Virgin Mary and Christ Child which she had originally gotten in Chios. Painted on the bottom of the left hand corner was a small picture of St. George slaying the dragon, and on the right hand corner at the bottom was a painting of St. Kyriaki. Between these two portrayals, were hand written letters that stated "by hand dimitriou x lambrinou". The artist's name is completely written in small letters, with no capital letters for the first and last names. The date, July 26, 1833. A silver replica of the icon covered it, obviously hammered by hand. The silver was covered in black, from the candle smoke of the votive offering. The size of the icon was eighteen inches high and thirteen and a half inches across. The date on the icon is July 26, 1839. There is a discrepancy on the date of the year, from the painting to the silver cover of six years.

All the children in the house were attracted to the icon because of its beauty, and the unusual silver covering. No one that we knew had such a beautiful religious object. However, there were also several other items from thea Venetia's dowry that elicited remarks of delight, with exclamations and requests that in the future, she might consider bequeathing to one of them.

She had, as was the Greek custom of the day, and any housewife would be sure to have, a silver cup with cutout silver figures on it. The top of it had small turrets, so that the spoons could be placed on the lip of the cup. The spoons were symmetrically twisted in the middle of the handle. There were also forks in the same pattern, to go with the spoons. There were twelve of each, and on the back of each was the stamp, Smyrna.

There were two round silver dishes to accompany the cup and spoons. They were used to put jelly in when serving guests. Thea Venetia also had an oval shaped serving tray, with a coffee pot. Those she had obviously gotten in the United States because their appearance resembled American made products.

The summer theo Niko bought his new Plymouth, he and Elia and Pete Vagen went to the Lake of the Ozarks for a few days. The following summer, theo Niko and thea Venetia asked us if we would like to drive and go for several days to the Lake of the Ozarks with them. Evangeline was almost six years old and Eliake was almost three years old. We stayed at the Pla-Port Resort, where Elia and I had stayed several times before. We had a pleasant time with them. Elia and theo Niko went fishing with Eliake.

In February of 1960, theo Niko was at Barnes Hospital. By that time diabetes had claimed both his legs, which had been amputated at the knees. He died in the hospital.

Thea Venetia was living at her home, with longtime friends to keep her company. She was also fortunate in that the woman who owned the flat that thea Venetia rented was Greek, and was of assistance to her.

Shortly before theo Niko died, he had two wills made out, one for her and one for him. His will left all their assets to her, and upon her death, to his relatives in Greece. He had named Ted Stamos as executor of the will. He had signed his will. Her will had the same stipulations. She had not signed her will. She had not agreed with him. A day after the funeral, she asked me to take her to the lawyer to change her will. His office was half a block from her home, on Grand Avenue.

She was going to leave the will in our favor, because as she told us, she only had a sister who was living in Greece. She did not know where, because they had not been in touch for many years, but she thought in Piraeus. I called the lawyer, and made an appointment for Friday afternoon, at four o'clock.

Unfortunately, snow had started falling during the day, and because she was old and had difficulty walking, and because I did not want to appear greedy, I called thea Venetia from school and told her we should change the appointment with the lawyer to Monday afternoon. She agreed.

Exactly a week to the day he died, on a Saturday night, Elia and I, with Evangeline and Eliake, were to spend the night at thea Venetia's. Elia and I were to go to the Greek Professional Club meeting and the children were to stay there with thea Venetia until we came home.

We went for dinner there. We sat in the kitchen around the table. She had cooked pork chops with spinach. While she was chewing on a piece of pork, she said, "This is very tasty". As she said that, her eyes rolled, and she slumped, and fell off her chair.

We quickly jumped up to help her. I told the children to go into the living room and wait. They held on to each other in the darkened room, afraid. I called the police emergency number. A heavy snow had begun to fall, with thick blinding flakes.

When the paramedics arrived, they pronounced thea Venetia dead. Unknown to us, her doctor, Dr. Vournas, had diagnosed her with a heart problem. She died of a heart attack.

I called Kyria Despina from upstairs. Then I called my mother to tell her the sad news. Thea Venetia died exactly a week to the day theo Niko died.

We made the funeral arrangements.

Constantinides family, 1946.

Fare Saved, Five Cents

One of the fondest memories of the Christmas holiday season of my childhood living on Aubert Avenue was going to downtown St. Louis to the two major department stores, the Famous-Barr Store on Sixth and Olive Streets, and to the Stix, Baer and Fuller Store on Washington and Seventh Streets to look at the animated window Christmas displays.

Going downtown to the Christmas displays was an event my siblings, Olympia, Platon, Johnny, and I looked forward to with great anticipation. For several years, I recall we went downtown with our cousins Joanna, Marie and Dessie and their mother, aunt Anna. They also lived on Aubert Avenue. Those trips were a real treat, even though winter had set in, and the weather was cold. Bundled up with wool caps, scarves, coats and gloves, we were oblivious of the winter temperature.

Using public transportation could be a problem and this was the time before my parents bought our first family car. In St. Louis in the mid-Thirties, street car and bus fares for adults were ten cents, for children under twelve years of age, five cents; and, for children under five years, there was no charge.

There were two street car lines, and one bus line near our house. The closest street car line was the Delmar line, running east and west. One block to the east of Aubert Avenue was the Taylor Street car line going north and south. One block to the west of our street was the Kingshighway bus line, also running north and south.

On Delmar Boulevard, the street car stopped at Aubert Avenue, so a person could board the street car, ride one block east and transfer to the Taylor streetcar or go in the opposite direction west one block and transfer to the Kingshighway bus with the same fare. As long as a person didn't backtrack, and continued on in another direction, the transfer was good.

On many occasions, when the Greek mothers we knew used public transportation to go any place in the city, to save a nickel, they had a child board the Delmar streetcar at Aubert Avenue, pay the nickel fare, get a transfer, and get off at the next corner. The adult would walk a block and meet the child at the corner.

This way a nickel was saved and the adult and the child would continue to their destination.

Those mothers were also resourceful in several other ways. They often managed to pass off the children who were over twelve years of age as under twelve years of age. Children who were already over five years of age could sometimes be passed as under five years, thus saving those fares as well. The children as a rule, hated being a part of the transfer routine, but obeyed and did it because they were aware that a nickel in those days was worth saving.

Another ploy those women developed was to have the mother who was the heaviest in weight, board the street car first. She stood before the conductor to pay her fare, thereby blocking his view. Then all the children would get on and go towards the back of the car. I recall we would look at each other, smile, and silently giggle and scoot down in our seats, so as to be as far away from the searching eyes of the conductor as possible.

On the occasion our combined family group was to go downtown to see the Christmas displays, my mother, my siblings, my aunt, my cousins and I walked one block east on Delmar Boulevard to Taylor Avenue. The children in our small group ranged in age from four years to fourteen years. As our little group waited, one of the mothers took two of the children, ages nine and ten, and walked one block south on Taylor Avenue. She waited for the Taylor car, and the two children got on. They paid the nickel child's fare, and each one got a transfer. They rode one block north to Delmar Boulevard, and got off. The mother walked the one block, and met them and the rest of the group. The transfers were then given to each of the adults. Our little, excited group then stood on the corner and waited for the Delmar car, going east in the direction of downtown, to come for us to board and begin our adventure.

How excited we all were to see the displays. The Christmas displays attracted many other people with small children too. We were ooh, oohing and ahhhing, pointing out the different features of the characters, pushing our way through the crowd of children and adults, jockeying for position to get the best view of the whole panorama. We commented on different parts of the display, what features we thought were good, which parts needed improvement. We marveled how ingeniously the whole display had been put together.

Each year, each department store featured a different Christmas theme. I recall one year the Famous store had planned their display around Clement Moore's poem, The Night Before Christmas. In the window display was a four poster bed with Mother and Father mechanical dolls, each wearing a nightcap that had a puff of yarn at the end. Father wore a yellow striped night shirt and Mother's nightgown was pink colored with small, dainty pink ribbons around the neck. They sat up in the bed, with jerky movements; Father stiffly getting out of bed to run to the window with sudden, twitching motions. There was a small portion of an overhanging roof in the display, covering Father as he peered out the window watching Santa Claus approach in the distance with Rudolph pulling his sleigh loaded with fancy wrapped gift boxes. There was a beautiful Christmas tree lit with blinking lights. There was even an animated brown mouse in the corner of the display, squirming in his hiding place, but never leaving it.

Not to be outdone by the Famous-Barr Christmas display, Stix, Baer and Fuller had a glittering Christmas display also. There was a huge enchanting Christmas tree, covered with small candles that were lit brightly and placed on the tips of the branches. The tree, covered with silver icicles, was in the middle of the display. Santa was on the side, sitting in an ornate silver covered throne, moving his arms about, occasionally kicking his feet up, nodding his head from side to side as deep sounds of "Ho, ho, ho" resounded.

There were four small animated models by the side of Santa Claus, two girls and two boys. The girls were dressed in ankle length gold and silver lace dresses that had stiff pinafore under-slips. Their hair was in tight Shirley Temple curls. The boys were dressed in blue velvet short pants, little Lord Fauntleroy suits that were all the rage at the time, with white satin shirts, and black velvet bow ties. All four figures twirled around and moved a few steps forward and back while Christmas carols played.

Not to be forgotten were the adult figures, their parents. The female figures were in beautiful evening gowns of the latest fashion and the male figures were in tuxedos.

An elaborately carved fireplace was in the background, with an artificial fire with burning logs. A cat and a dog lazily sat and watched the activity, their heads raised to survey the scene with jerking movements, and their tails periodically twitching.

There were crowds of people doing their holiday shopping, so the sidewalks were crowded and almost impassable. My mother and aunt Anna would take the smaller children by the hand, my sister Olympia being the oldest in the group would shepherd the rest of us as we managed to make our way through the masses of people to walk several blocks from one department store to the other.

Again we found ourselves faced with many other children trying to be first, to stand next to the window, to get an upfront view. Again the pushing and jockeying for a good view of the display. Tired, excited and exhausted by all the excitement of Christmas, the wonderful window displays, the crowds of people, we would begin our journey home. The same routine for the street car fares would be put into action, although the return trip and the saving of money was easier. There was a crowd of shoppers waiting to board the streetcar, and the larger group of people made it simpler for the children to get on the streetcar unobserved by the conductor.

Trips to see the department store Christmas displays held a magic for all of us, through our teen years, and even into adulthood. It was fun taking our own children downtown to see the displays, although for us, no public transportation was necessary. All we did was drive our car downtown!

Lost Money

In the worst years of the Depression, 1933 and 1934, I was nine and ten years old.

The dry cleaning business was very, very slow. In ordinary times, summer months were as a rule the slowest months of the year for the cleaning business because people did not usually wear clothes that required dry cleaning. But this summer, business was particularly slow because of the depressed economic situation.

On some days, the store was earning a few dollars, not much more than that. To economize, walking from the house on Aubert Avenue to the cleaners on Easton Avenue in the morning and walking home in the evening was routine to save money on carfare. The distance was three miles each way. Since we had no other transportation, no automobile, the distance was valiantly walked even after working in the store from eight o'clock in the morning to nine o'clock in the evening, a thirteen hour day. Very often, with my father was my mother or one of my siblings. I never heard my father or mother complain about the situation.

Fortunately, we had another source of income to see us through the slow business periods, the rent from the flat upstairs that we owned.

Sometimes I would walk the same distance, from our house to the cleaners, by myself. I knew the route, and even though I was so young, there was no risk to get lost. It was commonplace for me, I was familiar with the route. My family and I had walked the distance many times. I had no thoughts of fear.

One summer I walked to the cleaners to take my father his lunch. Later on a friend gave us a small two-wheeler bicycle that I used for that purpose. At that time my mother would put my father's lunch in a basket and strap it on to the small shelf above the rear wheel. I would then ride the bicycle to the cleaners, and take my father his lunch. I would ride north on Aubert Avenue a block to Fountain Avenue. I enjoyed riding down that street, admiring the two and three story homes. After turning right, ride four blocks to Lewis Place and through the Triumphal Arch. I enjoyed Lewis Place because it was a private street of well-kept homes, and with the many trees lining the sidewalk, I felt there was a leafy canopy above my head. I could ride all through Lewis Place, and the sun could not penetrate through the dense coating of leaves, to shine on me. The many trees and the thickness of the leaves blocked out the sunlight so that I rode in continuous cover of shade. I would emerge at Taylor Avenue, turn left and ride about four blocks to Easton Avenue, turn right, past the shoe store on the corner, past the dress shop, the restaurant, the grocery store, the empty store and then the cleaners, 4480.

I also took him his lunch several times when school was in session. During my lunch hour I would go home, quickly eat my lunch, and take the small basket with my father's lunch that my mother had prepared. I would walk north down Aubert Avenue to the street car stop, board the Hodiamont streetcar, which was at the end of our street, going east, and since I was under twelve years of age, my fare was a nickel. I would get off at Taylor Avenue, transfer to the Taylor line going north, and ride to Easton Avenue and the cleaners. After delivering my father his lunch, I would take the Wellston streetcar which ran on Easton Avenue, going west, again pay five cents fare, get off at Euclid Avenue and walk four blocks to Washington Elementary School to go to my classroom.

The only problem with that procedure was that it was not as efficient as we had hoped for. Several times my trip back to Washington School was slower than anticipated. When I got to school, the school yard was empty, the bell had rung, and the children were already in class. I was marked tardy for class by the teacher. Worse yet, I did not have a note from a parent explaining why I was late to enter my classroom. I bravely did go into the classroom late once or twice more, but then I became embarrassed to be late again. On the next occasion, seeing the school yard empty, and realizing I would be tardy again, I went home. After this happened for the second or third time, my parents abandoned the idea of my delivering my father his lunch on my lunchtime during the schoolyear.

On several occasions, in the summer, in addition to taking my father his lunch, he was to give me money so my mother could buy groceries. On one particular occasion, when I had walked to the cleaners to take my father his lunch, I found him alone in the store. That was usual at that time of day. It was cool inside, since the steam had not been turned on and the pressing machine was not working. Besides, the large, black ceiling fan overhead was stirring up a little cool breeze.

I stayed there for about an hour. My father ate his lunch. There was nothing for me to do there.

As I got ready to leave the cleaners, my father gave me a round, fifty cent piece to take home to my mother for groceries. I put the money in the pocket of my dress. I started the trip to go back home, going in reverse to the way I had come.

I recall playing on the way home, skipping in a few places, but did not stop anywhere, not even at Fountain Park with its refreshing and inviting water fountain.

When I finally got into the house, my mother was in the kitchen. She greeted me warmly. She asked me if my father had given me any money. I said yes, he had, fifty cents. I reached into the pocket of my dress for the fifty cent piece. It was gone! I had lost the money. There was no explanation. I had talked to no one, had not gone into a store, had not bought anything; nothing. I had played, though, coming back home, skipping on the sidewalk.

I had lost the fifty cent piece, the money my mother needed for groceries. The money I had gone to the cleaners to get. The money was gone.

My mother said nothing. She looked at me, and asked me if I was sure I didn't have it, perhaps I had overlooked it in my clothes. I searched my pockets again. No, I didn't have anything in my pockets. She did not yell at me, she did not scold me, she did not rant or rave, she did not punish me. Nothing. All she said to me was to be more careful next time.

Quietly, I left the kitchen and went and sat on the back porch, feeling sad, but feeling worse because my mother accepted my misdeed so graciously and I had failed her in an important mission.

Senior, Blewett High School, 1941.

Alex

Alex and Pete her brother lived in the two family flat next door to our home, on our left, number 763, in the second floor unit, on Aubert Avenue. Their parents owned the house. Their father owned a shoe shine store somewhere downtown.

Alex was about six months older than I. She started school the semester before me. In school, I was the better student, because in the early grades I passed her up when I received several double promotions. But in social situations she was more at ease, smiling, easy to converse with everyone. She and I were both talkative, and when we were together, we always enoyed each other's company. Physically we resembled each other a little. We were both dark, our hair was cut the same, bangs in front. We were the same height, and both were slightly chubby.

Alex and I played together all the time. One day, when we were both pre-schoolers, we were playing on the screened back porch of my house. My mother was in the front of the house, busy with her household chores. My sister Olympia was with her.

Alex and I decided to play Barber. I got a comb from the dresser in my mother's bedroom. We decided we needed a pair of scissors also. I went back into the bedroom where my mother had a treadle, foot driven Singer sewing machine. I pulled out a drawer on the side of the machine and found a pair of scissors. I went back to the porch and gave them to Alex who was patiently waiting for me. My mother and Olympia were still in the front of the house, unaware of what Alex and I were doing. We decided I would cut Alex's hair first. I took the scissors and started cutting her bangs. Her hair was straight, and the cutting I did, did not look very different from what her hair looked like when we started. There was a pan of water on the table on the porch, and I dropped her cut hair into the water. The strands of black hair were floating on top of the water.

Alex told me now she was going to be the barber. I quietly acquiesced. She proceeded to comb my hair, then took the scissors and decided to cut some of my bangs off. Since my hair was curly, Alex had trouble cutting it. She finally made some progress. I no longer had straight bangs across my forehead, but had skin showing through the gaps in my hair. She had me turn around, looked at me closely, and proceeded to cut big chunks of hair from the back of my head. She was having an equally hard time cutting my hair in back because of the curls. Some of the cuttings had missed the pan of water, and were now on the porch floor, and on the floor in the kitchen. We got tired of playing Barber so we decided to play Doctor. We went to play in the kitchen, under the table.

Just then Olympia came into the kitchen and saw us under the table. She stooped down to take a closer look at us, to see what we were doing. She saw black hair on the floor, took one look at me, and started shrieking at the top of her lungs, "Mama, mama, mama". At this unexpected turn of events, Alex started crying, got out from under the table, and ran out of the kitchen, through the back porch, down the steps, through the fence, and next door to her home. With Olympia's frantic screaming, my mother rushed into the kitchen to see what the commotion was about. She was visibly upset at what she saw, jagged wisps of hair hanging over my face, across the sides and the back of my neck. Instead of a hairline going straight across, she saw an irregular crude cut. She heard but did not see her neighbor's child rushing home in tears.

My mother was not a woman given to verbal eruptions or histrionics. Instead, she said in a calm voice, "It will be all right. Jennie's hair will grow out again," and the matter was closed. For my part, I was not perturbed in the least. Whatever mischief Alex had done to my hair was fine with me. To me, it was not of crucial importance. As my mother said, it would grow out again!

As far as Alex was concerned, I don't know if she ever told her mother what had happened. But my mother did not approach Alex's mother, or make an issue out of the incident. She merely let the matter close. After that hair-raising incident, for a little while Alex and I did not play together. Needless to say, when we did start playing together again, we were never allowed to play unsupervised.

Pete was older than Alex, and about a year older than my sister Olympia. In his early teens he was a typical boy, very active. There was a garage in their back yard, and one day playing with other boys, he climbed up on the roof of the garage. He tried to jump down, and broke his arm. At that time his mother had remarried, and to cover up his mischief, they told the stepfather Pete stumbled and fell from the front porch steps and broke his arm. In essence, Pete was mild mannered, happy, interested in gymnastics, and a good student. He eventually won a scholarship to the University of Indiana at Indianapolis. My mother was Pete's godmother, making us koumbari.

Their mother, Eleni, or as she was referred to, Eleniara, was from Smyrna. She was what is commonly referred to today as a nag. She was a constant nag to her husband, and children. An extremely domineering woman, she boasted with great pride that in her house the living room was out of bounds. No one was allowed to sit in the living room on her clean, slip-covered furniture, not even her husband, wishing to relax after a day's work at the cleaners.

She was a plain looking woman, certainly no beauty. Her hair was pulled back in a bun at the nape of the neck. I recall vividly many days when she would call from her back porch for her son who was playing with his friends, calling, in Greek, "Pete, ella thoe Pete". One of the non-Greek boys, Stanley Roche, took great delight in mimicking her, "Pete, ella doe Pete".

Her husband Paul was a short man. He worked long hours and wasn't home very much. Alex's mother and father were having financial problems. This was during the Depression when the economy was bad. The neighbors could hear them quarreling. The last time I recall seeing him was in the summer on a Sunday afternoon. I was about nine years old. Alex and I were sitting on my front porch playing with our dolls. Her father came walking down the street, and up their front steps. He opened the screen door, paused and said in a soft voice, "Alex, come home now". Alex picked up her doll, climbed over the fence, and went into her house.

That evening, just as it was getting dark, we heard screams from Alex's house. Pete came running down the steps, and went to a neighbor who had a telephone, to call an ambulance. The next morning we found out Alex's father was dead, a suicide. He had swallowed iodine. It was commonly whispered he could no longer cope with the negatives of his life. His shoe shining business was doing poorly, the constant nagging of his wife, her lack of understanding of his efforts of trying to eke out a living for his family, were more than he could bear. He left her with a paid up life insurance policy of a thousand dollars, plus the two family flat.

According to the 1930 census the house was worth $9,000. It had been constantly whispered someone would appear on the scene to marry her because, as a widow owning a house, she was a desirable prospect. Within six months Eleni had remarried. He was a tall, thin, gaunt Greek man who reminded a person what Abraham Lincoln must have looked like without his beard. His last name was Charbas, and he worked in a shoe factory. He was a kind, friendly man, born in mainland Greece. He was a very religious man, who scrupulously followed the religious holidays and fasted. He boasted he ate cheese and tomatoes when fasting.

In time we each went our own way. Alex married at the age of eighteen, and she and her husband Murphy moved away. Her stepfather Charbas died about a year later. Her mother Eleni sold the house, and moved in with Alex and Murphy. By that time Pete was in Indianapolis, at the University of Indiana. While a student at the university, Pete worked in a Greek restaurant. The owner had a daughter. Pete and she married and he remained in Indianapolis. We also sold our home a few months after Eleni sold hers, and we moved to 5021 North Kingshighway.

Tony, The Ice Cream Man

Among my most enjoyable memories of living on Aubert Avenue were the summer afternoons, when the heat and humidity of St. Louis prohibited playing hopscotch or jumping rope or roller skating on the sidewalk in front of the house. It was too hot to walk to Cabanne Library which was on Union Avenue and Cabanne Avenue, about a mile and a half from our house, with my sister Olympia, to borrow books by our favorite author Louisa May Alcott. Too hot even just to lay on the bed on the screened-in back porch.

But early afternoon was the best time to sit on the front porch with my sister Olympia, Bessie Laskaris, whose family lived in our flat upstairs, and Alex John, our neighbor from the house next door. Bessie was two years older than Olympia, and Alex was a year older than me. It was girl time. It was fun to sit on our front porch, and do grown-up, ladylike things like embroider pillow cases, crochet doilies; or do teen stuff like playing cards, Solitaire or Seven Card Rummy, or the board game of Monopoly. The boys did their own thing. My brothers Platon and Johnny were younger and playing in the back of the house, under the back porch, usually hammering away on some project of their own.

I secretly envied Bessie because she had the board game Monopoly which had just been put on the market for sale, and everyone raved about it. She had several other games besides. My siblings and I didn't have any board games. I wondered how Bessie could be so lucky to have games of her own. There was an older brother Nick, and Bessie, just two children in the family, whereas there were four of us, Olympia, Platon, Johnny and me. When Bessie would bring out the Monopoly game in her quiet and unassuming manner, the rest of us were pleased at the prospect of playing this newly popular game. We would childishly clap our hands, or exclaim happy thoughts at the arrival of the board game. We would always loudly proclaim how each one of us would use our playing skill to buy the most property, or encourage our luck to bring forth the correct combination of plays so we could be the winner.

My mother was usually home on those days of heat and humidity, because there was, as a rule, not much work for her at the cleaners during the summer months. Business was slow.

When Johnny was a toddler, Olympia and Bessie, on occasion, would wash him in the afternoon, dress him up, put him into the wagon, and take him up and down Aubert Avenue.

On certain days our little group, Bessie, Alex, Olympia and I, sat on the broad front porch, which stretched across the front of the house and was separated by a railing in the middle for the Constantinides and Laskaris sections. While we were occupied with quiet activities of handwork or serious concentration focused on playing our board games or cards, a friendly and welcomed sight came into view.

Down the street, at the corner, on our side of the street, a white painted, closed-in wooden cart, pulled by a horse, appeared. The horse wore a battered straw hat with two holes cut out in the brim for its ears to go through. Leaning out the window of the cart was Tony Loutas! Tony was Greek, a fact that I found quite interesting. Greek, and a vendor of my favorite treat, ice cream!

Tony was short, he had black hair, and always had a smile on his face, making his dark eyes laugh. My mother said Tony's wife was not Greek, and in my childish and innocent way, I tried to picture such an odd situation. His wife wasn't Greek? How could that be? All the Greek men my parents knew had wives who were Greek. Wasn't that always the case?

Tony was an entrepreneur, making and selling his own homemade ice cream. The price for a double dip ice cream cone was five cents. When one of us would spot Tony coming down the street, all activity ceased on the porch. Board game abandoned, embroidery and crocheting items left on the bench. We ran into the house yelling, "Mom, mom, Tony the ice cream man is coming! Can we get some ice cream?" My mother usually tried to please us, and would give us a deep bowl to take to him. She preferred to get the ice cream in a bowl, instead of giving us a nickel each to get a cone, even though the amount of twenty-five cents for a bowl of ice cream was equal to what she would have paid for five cones. She felt we were getting more ice cream for the money if we got it in bulk rather than for individual cones.

My mother would hand the bowl to Olympia, who as the oldest was the most responsible one of the four of us, and my sister would carefully walk down the porch steps, cognizant of her important mission. Then down the terrace steps to the sidewalk by the curb.

Slowly Tony's cart would make its way down Aubert Avenue, sometimes making a stop or two before it reached our house. We would stand and patiently wait for him to arrive at our place by the curb. Olympia would shyly hand him the bowl. Tony, with a smile, would take the bowl and fill it to the brim with scoops of the different flavors of ice cream that he had. Again, with a smile on his face, he would hand Olympia the filled container. She would pay him twenty-five cents, and turn around carefully so as not to drop the bowl and mount the steps going up the terrace to the porch.

I wondered if Tony obliged my mother's request for bulk ice cream as a special gesture of accommodation for her, or if he also did this for other Greek patrons, or for anyone else who might request it.

The horse would stand quietly by the curb as Tony took care of filling his orders. Other children would come down to the cart, stare or encircle the horse, cautiously pat it on the rump, or stroke it on the neck and watch with awe and amusement as it switched it's tail to get rid of flies that were annoying it.

My mother would generously fill four small bowls with ice cream for each of us. She tried to give us a scoop of each flavor from the large container; but we weren't particular. No one demanded a certain flavor, or pushed, or argued. We knew we would each get the same amount of ice cream. My mother did not play favorites and treated us equally. We sat quietly at our place at the table, anticipating the delight of the next few minutes. My mother kept very little ice cream for herself. For a little while, as we were in the kitchen enjoying our ice cream, we forgot all about the activity we had been pursuing on the front porch before Tony came. As it was, when we left, Bessie and Alex had also left the front porch.

My brother Johnny, when he was five or six years old, was thin. My parents felt he was a little too thin, and they should give him a little extra attention to help him to gain a little weight. Olympia and Platon remember that when my father would leave for work in the morning, he would specifically leave a nickel for Johnny to get an ice cream cone. Of course, my mother did not forget the rest of us.

Our cousin Marie remembers one time when she had a nickel and got an ice cream cone from Tony. The cone had the standard two scoops of ice cream. To her dismay, as she started to lick the top scoop, it slid off the cone and fell to the ground!

Tony's ice cream was always a treat for us to get because it was cheaper than the kind we bought at the drugstore fountain. Although Tony's ice cream was good, it was a little softer than the commercial variety. Regardless, it was a welcome treat, and for me, it made my day.

The Red And Gold Flowered China

As I sit at the beautifully arranged table enjoying Thanksgiving dinner, I am surrounded by happy grandchildren and their lighthearted parents. I look at the over-fifty year old china on the table. Only the wide red border and the slim gold line on the edge of the plate are visible. The flowers in the center of the plate are hidden by the half-eaten food. "Why are you so serious? What are you thinking?" my daughter Evangeline breaks in on my reverie. "Is something wrong?"

I smile, half-laughing. "No, I was just thinking, who could have thought, or imagined, over a half-century ago, we would still be using these plates."

My mind went back to the summer of 1938. I was fourteen years old, and the country was emerging from the Depression. Five doors away from my father's dry cleaning establishment on Easton Avenue in St. Louis was a small neighborhood theater, appropriately called the Easton Theater.

The building that housed the Easton Theater was brick, with no distinguishing architecture. It had no marquee, but there was a slender sign about ten feet high and two feet wide placed far up on the building with the letters placed vertically, spelling Easton. The cashier sat in a half-glass enclosure that was flush with the front of the building. The entrance to the theater reminded one of a dark, yawning mouth of a cave. There were no decorations on the walls; only a few glass framed posters displaying coming attractions. The rest of the walls were painted a dark color. There were very few lights in the lobby as we handed our tickets to the usher. Even the candy and popcorn stand looked forlorn, with very few items for sale, giving the impression as if they had been an afterthought.

The theater changed its bill of films every three or four days. First run films with such stars as Joan Crawford, Clark Gable, Robert Taylor would be shown along with an A Class and a B Class film. A cartoon or two were added to complete the program.

During the Depression years, the poor economy affected movie theaters along with other sectors of the business community. Throughout the hot summer months before the time of air conditioning, and at a period of time when movie goers preferred other forms of entertainment, the owners of the shows decided that an incentive was needed to induce people to attend the theater. In order to stimulate attendance some theaters offered glassware and others offered dinner dishes, free with the price of admission.

The price of admission was ten cents for adults, five cents for children. Only adults qualified to receive the free gift. However, if a child paid the full price of admission, he or she was also entitled to the free gift. Each week a different piece of china was offered: a cup, soup bowl, salad plate, dessert plate, dinner plate, bread plate, vegetable platter, meat platter. One piece for the price of one adult admission.

That summer, during the months of June, July and August we had a steady treat of going to the movies. We didn't miss a show. It was I who accidentally discovered this treasure that turned out to be a bonanza.

It was my mother's practice to go to the cleaners with Olympia to drive my father home in the evening. He would open the magazi in the morning at eight o'clock, and close in the evening at nine o'clock. He did not wish to leave the store any earlier in the evening for fear of missing any customer who might arrive and find the shop closed. He was also aware of the store directly across the street from our cleaners. The name on the plate glass window stated the name of the business, Sam the Tailor. Besides tailoring, Sam also took in cleaning of clothes, clearly in competition with us. My father, ever conscious of Sam's presence, would not close for the evening until he saw the lights turned off at Sam's. Then my father would announce to us, "We can close now. Sam has turned out his lights."

I would often drive down with them to pick up my father after his long workday. While waiting for my father to close up, I would walk the short distance to the show to see what films were playing and if any of my favorite movie stars were featured.

It was just such a time that I saw a special notice that china was being offered the following week. A sample platter was displayed. To me it was the most beautiful pattern I had ever seen on china, a wide red border with gold geometric design, and a slim gold line on the edge of the plate. There was a pink rose and a purple iris surrounded by yellow daisies, blue cornflowers and pink and blue morning glories gracing the center of the plate.

The theater was just completing a promotion of dark, smoky-colored Libby glasses. I knew that my mother had not been interested in those. She had more than enough glasses. But I walked back to the store excitedly and said, "Mom, come down to the show. Next week they are giving away dishes. They're very pretty, you'll like them."

My mother answered, not really interested, "We're almost ready to go home now, I can see them some other time."

"No, mom, come now", I pleaded. "It'll be just a minute, it's not far to go." With a reluctant look at my father, she said, "All right, just for a minute." Then she said, "We'll be right back."

We hurriedly walked the few steps to the show. My mother looked at the sample plate on display and her face broke into a smile.

"Very nice", she commented, "H-m-m, very nice. We don't really need dishes, but maybe we can come and get a few of these."

The truth was, we didn't need any more dishes. A few years before, after the christening of my youngest brother, my father bought my mother a complete new set of fine china. In the tradition of Greek celebrations, during the festive dinner after the baptism, happy guests and elated hosts alike threw dishes in joyful exuberance, a few at a time, crashing to the floor.

My parents, being Greek immigrants, enjoyed entertaining their friends in the same manner as if they were still living in the old country. They believed in having a good time.

The first piece of china that my mother got from our initial visit to the theater she inspected carefully. I turned the plate over, and read from the backside, "Royal Rajah Maroon, 22 K Gold, The Cronin China Co., Minerva, Ohio." There was also the stamp of a union label, National Brotherhood Operative Potters.

That summer, and for almost every film showing, two or three times a week, my mother would pile my sister, my two brothers, me, and herself into Henry, our two-door, blue Ford, and Olympia would drive us to the Easton Theater. My father didn't attend the movies with us because of the confining hours of the cleaners. He also had to revert to public transportation to go home, the streetcar.

My mother would buy five adult admission tickets, and then hand the tickets to the usher at the entrance. He in turn would reach into a corrugated cardboard box perched on a chair by his side, and hand each of us our piece of china. For certain pieces that my mother desired more of, she would also recruit my two cousins for that mission. This way she was sure of getting the desired number of a particular item.

No piece of china was ever broken. My mother would thoughtfully bring a brown paper bag with her. In the darkened theater, she carefully placed the china in the bag, and then placed it under the hard, wooden seat on the floor where the china would be safe until it was time to go home.

In this manner, our family managed to accumulate place settings for twenty-two people. For the serving platters, vegetable and meat and for the salt and pepper shakers, the project was scaled down accordingly since too many pieces were not required. On those occasions only a few adult tickets were bought from the cashier, the remainder of the tickets were for children.

As the years progressed, the Depression dishes became her good china for company and special occasions. The set my father had gotten for her years before took second place. The red-gold border, the colorful flowers in the center of the plates made an attractive setting with her fine crystal and lace tablecloth.

The china graced my mother's table for many successive Thanksgivings, Christmases, Easters and a host of other occasions. She never seemed to run out of dishes as the guests seated at the table over the years went from the six of us to an expanded and extended nineteen. The only casualties to the china over the years were the cups. For some reason, they were not able to withstand frequent use. There are only five cups now left.

My mother used those dishes to the very end of her life.

My daughter Evangeline, in the many years of visiting her grandmother, admired the dishes greatly. Often she would remark to her grandmother, for whom she was also named after, "Yiayia, when I get married, I want you to give me these dishes." And Yiayia would remark, "Evangeline, they are yours, no one else can have them." The china set survived the move intact from St. Louis to Kent, Ohio. My daughter, now in her own home, has her own set of fine china. However, she still maintains the red and gold flowered plates and the Thanksgiving tradition begun by her grandmother over a half-century ago. "Evangeline," I said to my daughter at the end of the meal as we carefully cleared the table of the heirloom plates from the Easton Theatre, "Yiayia knew you loved these dishes. She must be very pleased, knowing you cherish and are using her precious china in your own home."

Dandelions

Looking back on my childhood in St. Louis on Aubert Avenue, I had many happy experiences. However, one activity in the early and middle Thirties, that I was not very fond of, was going with my mother and gathering dandelion greens.

Spring was usually greeted with enthusiasm by my parents, because it signaled the season that dandelion greens had arrived. They were a favorite of my parents. Dandelion greens were not available in grocery stores, and in Greek and Mediterranean cooking, they are considered a great delicacy.

Before we got our car Henry, the blue '37 Ford, which expanded our dandelion trips, my mother would get big, brown kraft paper bags and knives, and walk to Fountain Park which was just a block away from our house. My mother would take my sister Olympia and me with her.

This was usually in the Spring before the yellow flower of the dandelion had had a chance to bloom and its leaves grow bitter. Dandelions are an excellent source of vitamin A and some B vitamins. Low in calories, they contain protein, calcium, iron, sodium, phosphorous and a decent amount of vitamin C, magnesium and potassium. I believe the feeling was that the leaves were more tender to eat before the plant had a chance to flower.

Fountain Park was an oval shaped park, and it stretched from Aubert Avenue east, past Euclid Avenue to Bayard Avenue. At the park's widest point, which was at Euclid Avenue, there was a beautiful fountain with the water splashing and often overflowing its base. Here the width of the park was less than a half a block wide. There were beautiful large, brick, two-story houses flanking each side of the park. The homes had long front porch verandahs.

My mother would usually walk up and down the park, looking for the tenderest young plants.

When she was satisfied that she had found the best dandelion greens available, she would take a knife, bend down, cover the tender young plant with her left hand, grasp it firmly, slice the plant with her right hand and yank it up out of the ground. She would shake it gently to get as much dirt out of the leaves as possible; slice off any of the root that may have remained, and then put the cut plant in the bag. When my sister and I first started to go with our mother to gather dandelions, she let us try our hand at pulling up the dandelion plant out of the ground. I suppose she thought that method was safer for us than trying to use a knife. However, soon we were promoted to using a knife also.

Our dandelion ventures were not restricted just to Fountain Park. My brothers Platon and Johnny also remember going to Forest Park, on Kingshighway and Lindell Boulevards, to gather dandelions. That was after we had gotten our car Henry. My mother or my sister would drive us, and my mother would invite several of her friends to come also. The ladies were quite pleased to be asked to join the adventure, because besides the opportunity to socialize with each other, the dandelion greens would be a welcome addition to any meal, and the price was right. It was felt that in such a large area as Forest Park, there were many more dandelion greens to be found than in any other local area. Much to the disappointment of our friends, grocery stores did not sell these greens.

The ladies brought their standard equipment: big brown kraft paper bags and knives. With the knife in one hand and the big bag on the ground, the ladies, with much enthusiasm, cut the dandelion plants, shook off as much dirt as possible, and placed the leaves in the bag.

When the bags were full, they got in the car and we went home.

Johnny recalls playing in the park as my mother and her friends filled up their bags. One of the things Johnny remembers on those dandelion trips to Forest Park was the fountain at the entrance to the park on Kingshighway Boulevard. The fountain had four spouts of water running continuously. If you stopped up one spout, the other spouts shot up higher. He would plug up three spouts and the water out of the fourth spout shot up very high. If he tried to stop all four spouts, the water would squirt out from all four. He always enjoyed watching the water.

It wasn't just the women at Forest Park who were interested in gathering dandelion greens. Platon remembers going with our neighbor, Kyrio Yorgie (Laskaris) who rented and lived with his family on the second floor of our two-family flat. Platon recalls going with Kyrio Yorgie on Sunday mornings to the Delmar Wabash train depot located at Delmar, Kienlen and Skinker Avenues that bordered the western city limits of St. Louis. The trains went underground at Delmar Boulevard, but up to that point, the sides of the train tracks were like the side of a small hill. Above the incline, the ground became level.

In the spring this piece of level ground was covered by dandelion plants. It is difficult to determine how or who discovered this site, but Platon and Kyrio Yorgie, armed with their six to eight brown shopping bags with handles, and with their knives, were able to gather and completely fill up their bags with greens. It was a trip well worth the cost of the fare for they went by streetcar, riding to the Delmar Wabash train site. The street car fare was ten cents for adults and five cents for children, one way. A successful endeavor indeed.

I was at times apprehensive about collecting dandelions. As I got older, I became self-conscious of what people passing by would think, as they saw, women armed with small knives and brown bags, as far as they could tell, cutting weeds out of the ground and saving them. Middle-aged women, slightly plump, each with her hair pulled back in a tight bun at the base of the neck, speaking a foreign language. A bunch of small children running around playing. I was not aware that any other people would even take a second look at dandelions as food. I hoped that no one who knew me from school would see me.

When we got home with our brown bags full of dandelion greens, we had to wash them carefully, rinsing them several times to get out all the dirt. Then my mother would boil them. When cooked, she would serve them with olive oil and lemon juice. They had a slight bitter taste, but even so, they were delicious. When I became an adult, I learned many other people, non-Greeks, knew about dandelions, and even made wine out of the yellow flower!

Truck Ice

Before electric refrigerators were invented in the early Thirties, housewives kept their perishable foods in an icebox. Just as the name implies, it was a box made of wood, about four feet high, for ice. It had two doors. On one side, the door opened where the ice was placed, and on the other side, the door opened to reveal several shelves accommodating different articles of food. On the bottom of the icebox a pan was placed to catch the water dripping from the ice as it slowly melted. Every day the pan had to be emptied of water, and each day the ice had to be replaced by either a twenty-five pound piece of ice or a fifty pound piece.

In the summer, a truck would drive down the street in the morning to deliver ice to the different homes. Housewives would place a card in their front room windows, designating the amount of ice they wanted that day, twenty-five or fifty pounds. If the card was not in the window, the driver of the ice truck would check back the next day.

Usually there was a group of boys gathered around the ice truck, for as the driver chipped off the different amounts of ice from the large slab of ice, chips of ice would fall on the truck, or off the truck, and the boys would fight to get those pieces.

Our iceman was Greek. He was a friendly man, about thirty-five to forty years old. He also had a farm somewhere in Illinois, not too far from St. Louis.

Several times, our iceman friend invited the Greek people living on Aubert Avenue to go to his farm for a picnic. Since none of the families had a car, he volunteered to take us on his truck; about four families with children; about fifteen people altogether, took advantage of the iceman's offer. Each family brought a picnic basket. I believe the picnic was on a Sunday. Everyone had to climb up on the bed of the truck, my mother, sister Olympia, brothers Platon and Johnny, and I. We all had to sit on chairs or on boxes.

Our Greek friend drove us to his farm. We stayed all day. We had a good time. Then in the evening he drove us all back home to Aubert Avenue.

Stefan and Evangelia with Olympia and Jennie, 1926

Maro

I have many memories from my childhood in St. Louis more than six decades ago when my family lived on Aubert Avenue as one of fifteen Greek immigrant families. At the time I was unaware of the comfortable, enduring feelings living in such an environment had on me. There were times, of course, when the strong ethnic bonds had its drawbacks. Good behavior was the cardinal rule, because it was unacceptable to a Greek family to become embarrassed in the neighborhood. Growing up with the warmth and familiarity of Greek people, however, made for positive and long-lasting experiences for me.

Aubert Avenue was in the West End of the city. It was a middle-class neighborhood, of two family brick flats, with a few single family, two story homes, also constructed of brick. After a devastating fire in St. Louis, towards the end of the nineteenth century that burned wooden buildings on many streets, an ordinance had been passed in the city that declared all future construction was to be composed of brick. The street of Aubert itself was level, but some homes were built on a slight terrace. To reach my house it was necessary to go up the terrace about twelve steps to the sidewalk and the porch, then up another six steps to the front door. In the 1920's, the street was laid with bricks and years later, black-topped. Beautiful, large-leafed sycamore and small-leafed silver maple trees lined the street.

Almost all of the Greek families had come from Asia Minor. The men were self-employed, small business men, owning barbershops, restaurants, a shoe repair shop, or they were hatters and cleaners. Most of them had arrived before World War I, either to avoid service in the Turkish army or to work and send money back to their families. Most of the women came later, refugees from the 1922 Smyrna Catastrophe, who married men who had gone to Greece looking for a wife. My parents fit in neither category. They had come to the United States in 1919 on their honeymoon, to stay a few years, and then return to what they thought would be a comfortable life in Smyrna. However, because of the Catastrophe, that was not to be, so my parents accepted their fate, and adjusted to life in their adopted country, not lamenting the life they had left behind. Some of the wives who had married in Greece while they were refugees, however, lived in St. Louis with memories of Smyrna, and the life they had once had.

Evangelos and Katherine Pasmezoglu and their daughter Maritza had arrived in the United States in 1912, from Smyrna. At that time, the Father was fifty-eight years old, the mother fifty years old and Maritza was nineteen years old. After the death of Mr. Pasmezoglu, twenty years later around 1932, Mrs. Pasmezoglu and Maritza moved to Aubert Avenue. Maritza by then was in her late thirties.

The Pasmezoglu family had come to the United States because their three sons, Hector, Epaminondas and Miltiades were already here, and each one was financially secure. It was a well-known fact among the fifteen Greek families on Aubert Avenue that the Pasmezoglu family had been a distinguished and aristocratic family in Smyrna, prominent and wealthy. They had been in the silk manufacturing business.

Hector was the oldest of the three Pasmezoglu sons and had come to the United States just before the 1904 St. Louis World's Fair on business. By the time his parents and sister came, he was a well-established business man and was married to Penelope, the daughter of Father Phiambolis, one of the first Greek priests in St. Louis. Hector was also the Greek consul in St. Louis. He was coordinator of the Olympic Games at the 1904 World's Fair. He was the president of the Acorn Supply Company, and in the theater business with the Skouras brothers. He had a home on Forest Park Boulevard, a neighborhood which then was considered very upper middle class. St. Nicholas Greek Orthodox Church was built on the lot next to his home. Years later, the church bought his home and used it as an office and Sunday School building. His wife Penelope was president of the Mozart Amusement Company.

Miltiades had arrived in the United States in 1910 at the age of thirty. He became a naturalized citizen in 1919. He was an insurance salesman. He was a pleasant and very likable man. He loved an American woman, so it was said, but his mother refused to accept her into the family and he never married. He contracted an illness, which in time infected his brain, and he had to be institutionalized in a state asylum. He never recovered from his devastating illness and died in the asylum.

Epaminondas went by his Americanized name of Edwin. He was also married, and in 1920 was treasurer of the Mozart Amusement Company. Later, in the Thirties, he was in the exterminating business. His company had a promisng business, and did very well. They were established in St. Louis for many years. His mother and sister were proud of his accomplishment, but later Epaminondas moved away from St. Louis and went to another city to continue his business there.

According to the 1921 City Directory: Edwin, Treasurer Mozart Amusement, lived at 4120 Enright Avenue. Kathy and Evangelos, Milton, lived at 715 North Euclid Avenue. Hector, President Acorn Supply, lived at 4967 Forest Park Boulevard with his wife, Penelope, President Mozart Amusement. A descendent, Perry Pasmezoglu, born Dec. 13, 1910, died Dec. 1984. Residence, Los Angeles, Calif..

My parents were friends with Mrs. Pasmezoglu and her daughter Maritza. At that time they were renting the first floor of a two-family flat down the street, four doors from our home. The two women made a lifelong impression on me.

On many a humid, sweltering St. Louis summer afternoon, when I happened to pass their house, I would see the mother and daughter sitting in their rockers on the wide verandah porch. Fanning themselves with hand held paper fans, they talked to each other and observed the activity on the street.

The mother, Mrs. Pasmezoglu, was a domineering, temperamental, controlling woman, who demanded blind obedience from her daughter Maritza whom she called Maro. Maro served her like a slave.

Maro had been proclaimed a stunning beauty when she had come to St. Louis. She had classical Greek features. The Greek neighbors were curious that she was a spinster, and could not understand why she had never married.

Maro could be described as a sweet, dutiful daughter but could also be termed a little dull in intelligence. Maro's limited faculties were obvious to everyone. Mrs. Pasmezoglu had explained her daughter's mental failing by saying that Maro had had a serious childhood illness, the effect of which left her a little dimwitted.

Mrs. Pasmezoglu lived in the past. Her conversation, spoken softly in beautiful and correct Greek, consisted of stories of her social life in Smyrna. The prominent people she knew. The servants she had. She would mourn her fate, of losing her riches, to come to this end.

Very often, during Mrs. Pasmezoglu's reminiscences, Maro would ask her mother in an innocent and sincere manner, "Mama, ego to thimame afto?" (Mama, do I remember that?). Without fail, the answer would invariably be, emphatically, "Oxi, Maro, esi eisouna poli mikri." (No, Maro, you were too young). In many, many instances according to her mother, Maro was always "poli mikri." (too young).

Maro was no longer a beauty when she became our neighbor. The years of serving her mother, the neglect of herself, had taken a toll on her appearance. Her hair was still all black in color, and she wore it pulled back in a bun at the nape of her neck, as was the custom of most Greek women of that time. She was already round shouldered, with a slight hump on her back. Her figure was matronly, and she walked with a slow, absentminded gait. She had large, sagging breasts. Her mother explained that by saying when Maro was a teenager, and her body was just beginning to develop, her breast had been tightly bound to keep it small. However, the opposite evidently had occurred.

All the Greek children on the street were taught to respect every Greek adult as if they were their parent. This was the era when respect for elders was foremost in the behavior of the children of the Greek immigrant, even though several of the bolder, daring teenaged Greek boys would caustically refer to the mother as Mrs. Pass-me-the-glue.

For me, I had a feeling of dread about Mrs. Pasmezoglu. Perhaps it was her imperious manner, I felt she might find some fault with me and tell my parents. Or perhaps it was the atmosphere of her home, which always appeared dark and a little forbidding, that intimidated me and made me feel a little anxious. I recall going to Mrs. Pasmezoglu's home, and listening to her as she would go into great detail about the beautiful home and the servants she had in Smyrna. She never tired of relating and reliving tales of her Asia Minor social life.

Later, when I was at home, I would imitate her, wave my arms, and pronounce to my audience, "to enter my front door, you had to pass two majestic sculpted lion statues, one on either side of the steps. They were grand examples, made of stone. They looked almost real." I would laugh, pleased with myself at such a performance.

In the Pasmezoglu dining room there was a china closet, and I remember Maro pointing out with pride the hand painted china dishes one of her sister-in-laws had painted. In those days, one of the marks of the well bred young woman was the accomplishment of this activity.

I had noticed a large black trunk in one of the rooms in the home, and one day when I was there, Maro raised the lid. I had often wondered what mysterious things she and her mother had hidden in that trunk. To my surprise and delight, Maro took out beautiful, elaborate vaudeville costumes. I was awed and impressed by such clothes. They were from the Uptown Theater down the street, a block away on Delmar Boulevard, that Hector owned. The Uptown Theater had been converted from a vaudeville show to a moving picture theater. It no longer had stage shows or the need for such costumes. What, I wondered, would they do with such items? To my childish mind, they would have been great to dress up in them and play House, or to imagine myself wearing them as a queen or princess in a fairy tale.

When we got our Norge refrigerator during the Depression, around 1932, we were the only Greek family on Aubert Avenue to have one. We happily discarded our wooden icebox. No longer did my Mother have to put the numbered card in the front window for the ice truck delivery man to see how many pounds of ice we needed for that day. No longer did we have to daily empty the pan under the icebox that caught the melting ice and then empty the water into the sink, being careful not to spill any water on the linoleum covered kitchen floor. That was a difficult chore.

Our new refrigerator was one of the earliest models that had the capability of making ice cubes. Maro would come with a container to get ice cubes. My mother would oblige Maro, and direct either my sister or me to get the ice cube trays out of the refrigerator, and fill Maro's container. As I turned my back on the adults to go to the refrigerator to get the ice cube trays, I often made a face to show my irritation of having to obey my mother. I was careful that neither adult saw my reaction.

Maro had the habit of coming to our house by the back way, down the alley from her house to ours. She never came to the front door to ring the doorbell or to knock on the door. She preferred the back way. No matter what time of day, or what season, summer or winter, spring or fall, it was the back way. Whether we were playing in the yard or on the large back screened porch, we could easily see her enter the back gate, lumber up the five steps from the alley to the side-walk, and then slowly walk through the back yard to the porch steps. Maro never rushed or walked fast. She moved slowly.

Whenever any one of us saw her approaching, we would run through the house yelling, "Maro is coming, Maro is coming." We knew what that meant. When Maro would reach the screen door on the porch, she wouldn't bother to knock, she would call out, "Evangelia, Evangelia" for my mother, then open the screen door and walk right into the kitchen. We knew Maro's presence meant we would be involved with something and we viewed that with very little enthusiasm.

Our mother always treated Maro and her requests graciously. She would tell us, "Kane to kalo, kai xehaseto" (Do the good deed, and forget about it). She felt sorry for Maro and her mother, and accommodated their requests. She would often remind us that they were two women living alone in their house, struggling with their problems without the help of a man.

The task of running Maro's errands fell on my sister or me. Maro would never approach any other Greek family to have their children run errands for her. She knew my mother was compassionate and would oblige her. Some of the other

Greek mothers were not so sympathetic or accommodating. Maro would come to our house for either my sister or me to go to the Cap-Sheaf Bakery on Kingshighway Boulevard, two blocks away, to buy day old whole wheat bread for a nickel a loaf. Or to go to Kroger's grocery store at the corner of the Hodiamont tracks and Kingshighway Boulevard to buy some item for her.

Olympia and I used to hate to go to the store for Maro, and when she would leave our house, whichever one of us went, would grumble and complain about it to our mother. But our mother just ignored our complaints. Basically, we had no recourse but to do as we were told by our mother, whether we liked it or not.

When Maro and her mother arrived in St. Louis, and Maro was still young and beautiful, many Greek suitors pursued her. But while her mother lived she never married because Mrs. Pasmezoglu felt no one was good enough for her daughter. They were unworthy to become a member of such a distinguished family.

One of the wealthiest Greeks of the time, John F. was in love with Maro, and wanted to marry her. He had been a shepherd in Greece, a very poor boy. After he came to the United States, he was able to start his own business, a successful meat packing plant, situated across the Mississippi river from St. Louis in Madison, Illinois. At one time he was considered the wealthiest Greek in St. Louis. He was very active in the church and was one of the founders of St. Nicholas.

At a dinner party in an elegant restaurant in the Chase Hotel with John F., attended by Maro and her family, Maro's napkin fell to the floor, and the suitor failed to pick it up. Maro's mother was infuriated, and dismissed the young man as unsuitable, "aftos o choriatis, o chobanis", (that villager, that shepherd), having no manners, was not for her daughter.

After serving her mother like a slave all those years, around 1942, the old lady died. Our family was still living on Aubert Avenue when Maro's niece came and helped her move to a small apartment near St. Nicholas, the Greek church. Maro, now in her early fifties, and free of parental domination for the first time in her life, with her limited ability, had to learn to cope with the difficulties of everyday living. Word got out that Maro's lifestyle had changed. She started smoking and drinking. Her scandalous behavior was observed by Greek people in her new neighborhood, carousing and frequenting bars. Everyone was appalled at her behavior. "Ti tropis, ti tropis!" (What a shame, what a shame!), was the common remark from the old neighbors on Aubert Avenue when Maro's current behavior became common knowledge.

Maro married, without consulting anyone, an old, down and out, shiftless Greek man. She and her newly acquired spouse lived in her rented, small apartment. People said he married her because he thought she had money. Actually, she had nothing. Her married life was of short duration. She died not too many years after her wedding.

A pitiful, sad ending to the promise of a life that might have been. Born into a family of wealth and prominence, she became a victim of familial arrogance, domination and interference. A victim.

Maro, another victim to the temperamental twists of life's eternal caprices.

Evangelia with Jennie, 1938

Mission Accomplished

The first home my parents owned, where I and my two brothers were born, was the two family flat at 761 Aubert Avenue. My sister had been born a few years earlier at 4724a Olive Street.

In those days, my father owned a dry cleaning store in partnership with another Greek man, Nestora Papaspanos. Before the Depression, the store was doing very well. It did enough business to support two families nicely, ours and the partner's. My father and Nestora each worked half-days.

With the painful economic decline of the Depression, in the Thirties, it was decided my father would borrow on his John Hancock life insurance policy to buy out his partner, since the economic downturn had affected the business and the store now would support only one family. We had enough money for our daily food and expenses, plus the additional income from the rent from the flat upstairs, which was paid promptly every month. However, there was not enough money left over to pay the monthly note on the house mortgage. For almost two years, no house payment was made.

Our family began to emerge from the financial setback of the Depression about 1934. By that time, my mother had convinced my father to allow her to work at the cleaners doing alterations. She would stay home during the day, cook the meals, and do her housework. When my older sister and I came home from school at 3:30 in the afternoon, she would leave for the cleaners. My sister would baby sit my two younger brothers, ages four and two, and me, everyday including Saturday, until my parents came home at 9:30 in the evening.

Eventually, my parents were able to and wanted to resume mortgage payments on our home. We had been extremely fortunate in that the mortgage lender, a woman, had not demanded payment or foreclosed on the property. Either way, it would have been a losing proposition for her because the real estate market was so depressed and glutted with foreclosed property, the flat would have been a liability on her hands. Property was just not selling.

My mother convinced my father she should take me with her to the real estate company and tell the realtor to contact the holder of the mortgage to completely write off the two years of non-payment of interest. My parents would resume again the monthly payments. Since my mother spoke no English, my function would be interpreter. My sister had to baby sit my younger brothers. I was considered proficient in the matter of translating the two languages, English and Greek, even though I was only ten years old.

My father was shocked. Stunned. It was unbelievable to him that the mortgage holder would even agree to such an outlandish suggestion. However, my mother's mind was made up, she would not be deterred from accomplishing her objective.

One afternoon when I came home from school, my mother took me and we walked to the Botorff Realty Company. It was only two blocks away, on Delmar Boulevard past Euclid Avenue, next to the West End Lyric Theater. The realty company was in a storefront office. On the large plate glass window, facing the street the name Botorff was printed in large gold letters in a half-moon, and below it in a straight line, the word Realty. As my mother and I entered the office, Mr. Botorff was alone, sitting at a high roll top desk. I noticed he was a tall, thin man. He wore glasses, and there was a smile on his face. He was a man of a pleasant disposition and I had no reason to alter that impression after our conference with him. He said to us "Come in, come in ladies. How can I help you?"

My mother said to me in Greek, "Tell him our name, where we live, and that we want to talk about paying on the mortgage of our house."

I was not confident in initiating projects, but guided by someone else, in problems of negotiations, I did very well. I could easily follow directions. In English, I bravely related our mission.

Mr. Botorff smiled and said, "Fine, let me get the file and we'll see what there is to be done." He went to a green filing cabinet, opened a drawer, rifled through it, and took out a manila folder. He smiled at us as he came back to his desk and said, "Well, here we are." Then he broke off with a puzzled look on his face, saying, "Oh, yes, now I remember. No payment has been made for some time, almost two years to be exact."

I relayed the information in Greek to my mother. She said "Tell him I know that. That 's the reason we are here." Once again I interpreted and gave the message to Mr. Botorff. He said, "Yes?"

I looked at my mother. She said, "Tell him to get in touch with the holder of the mortgage and tell the lady to forget about the unpaid interest of the last few years. Tell him to tell her we will start paying next month again, the new interest."

I had no great idea about money, let alone knew anything about payments or interest. I didn't know the relevancy of the statement or its impact. I did as I was instructed. I relayed the message I was given. All during my recitation, the realtor kept shaking his head from side to side, side to side. After a prolonged moment of silence, he finally said, "No, that cannot be done. Impossible."

My mother understood his reaction without my clarification. She said, "Tell him to approach the lady. She will agree to it." I repeated my mother's proposition. Again the head shaking, the moment of meditation, and the answer, "No, it cannot be done. Impossible." Again the request, "Tell him to approach the lady. She will agree to it."

Whether Mr. Botorff recognized that my mother would not be put off and that she was definitely adamant in her request, or whether he felt such a request was legitimate, or whether he felt he should give up and call it a day, he wearily shrugged his shoulders and said, "All right, I will call the lady and ask her to do as you ask. We'll see how she feels about this idea. I will let you know."

At that, my mother stood up from her chair. I followed her lead. She instructed me to thank the kind gentleman. They shook hands and we left the office. On the way home my mother's feet seemed to have wings. I could feel the lighthearted steps matching her lithesome air.

My mother went on to work at my father's cleaners, and I stayed home with my sister and brothers. I don't know what my father's verbal reaction was to my mother's visit to the realty office, but that evening when they came home from work, my father was very quiet. For the rest of the evening, as I looked at him, I thought I saw a half-smile on his face, a feeling all was well with the world.

One afternoon about a week later, when my sister and I came home from school, my mother was waiting at our front door for us. In her excitement, she thrust a letter from Mr. Botorff to both of us. "Read, read this and tell me what it says", she said to us, urgency strong in her voice.

Quickly, we simultaneously read aloud the letter, and started yelling happily. "Mom, mom, it's okay," I said. "It's okay. Mr. Botorff said the lady said it's okay, you don't have to pay the money you missed for the last two years! It's okay!"

That evening, when my parents came home from the cleaners, I can't recall seeing two happier people. A difficult and unusual mission had been accomplished. My father was beaming from ear to ear. My mother was quietly pleased with herself. They looked and acted like two people very much in love and in love with the world.

Swimming

During the early Thirties, at the beginning of the Depression years, Olympia, Platon, Johnny and I were still in our childhood and living on Aubert Avenue. For us, and for all of our friends living on our street, with the end of the academic school year in June, a very pleasant experience awaited us. We anticipated and eagerly looked forward to Vacation Bible School.

Vacation Bible School was held at a church on the corner of Kingshighway Boulevard and Cabanne Avenue. It was free of charge to all who attended. The location of the church was well within our walking ability. On a bright, sunny morning, as we walked north on Aubert Avenue, we were joined along the way by our friends and cousins, singing, laughing, all in a happy mood. We proceeded on Aubert Avenue, in the shade of the large leafed sycamore trees, to the end of the block to Fountain Avenue, then turned left and walked a short block to Kingshighway Boulevard. The church was directly across the street on the west side of Kingshighway, and holding each other's hands, we carefully crossed the busy thoroughfare.

The church was an impressive building, built of gray stone, very solid. It was not an ostentatious looking edifice, and yet not a plain building either. I can't clearly recall the name of the church, but I think it was called Kingshighway Presbyterian Church.

Vacation Bible School was a treat for our group, because, even though it was a school, it was not so in the traditional sense, with a core curriculum to be followed as in the public school. It's purpose was religion, and attendance required was only for half a day. The school was in session only several weeks. It afforded us the opportunity to not only have somewhere to go for a period of time in the summer, which our parents appreciated, but the real attraction of Vacation Bible School was going swimming!

The church had an indoor swimming pool. The pool was an unexpected treat, available to all the children attending Bible School. At that time, it was the only opportunity for the neighborhood children to swim in an authentic swimming facility. There was no other one available in the area. It became the high point of our summer. We eagerly went to Vacation Bible School, in large measure for the rare opportunity of swimming in a real pool. Outside of the Forest Park Highlands Amusement Park (which was on the other side of Forest Park and a distance of roughly six miles away from our homes, requiring public transportation), there was no other swimming facility available.

The teachers and personnel of the church were kind and gracious to all the children, regardless of religious affiliation. Olympia remembers that every morning, all classes were begun with the singing of the song, Jesus Loves Me. All voices were raised in anticipation of a pleasant morning. Never were we questioned about our religious beliefs, even though we were a mixture of Jewish, Catholic, Protestant and Greek Orthodox.

The classrooms of the school were in the basement of the church. The entrance was from the outside of the church by the stairway leading to the lower level. It was on the Kingshighway side of the building. We descended about eight steps to reach the door to enter the school. The schedule for swimming, as Platon remembers it, was that girls and boys were not allowed to swim together. The girls swam on two different days, and the boys swam on two different days. In that period of time, all girls wore the proper swimming attire regardless of age, a one piece bathing suit; bikini swimming outfits had not entered the fashion scene yet. Johnny recalls that there was a strict rule that anyone with an open sore, or a cut, was not allowed to swim.

On our way home from Vacation Bible School we carried our wet bathing suits wrapped up in our towels. Some of the children carried their parcels as if they had won a trophy. Everyone was happy, feeling good. Our mothers welcomed us with joy on seeing us in a happy frame of mind and very pleased that we had had a good morning. After eating our lunch, and helping our mother clean up the table, we would go to the large screened back porch, get our favorite library book, and lay down on the daybed to read.

However, our swimming horizons expanded in the late thirties after my parents bought our second car, the 1937 blue Ford, Henry. By that time Olympia had learned to drive, and our swimming knowledge had expanded. We had heard that there was a very good outdoor swimming pool in Heman Park in University City. It was owned and operated by the city. Whenever we drove by the pool we got a good impression; we saw people having fun.

University City was an upscale affluent area in St. Louis County, adjacent to the City of St. Louis, with large homes and well kept tree shaded lawns. All who attended the pool had to pay an entrance fee, but by the late 30's, business at our cleaners had picked up and the cost of admission to the swimming pool was no problem. Of course, my father never accompanied us on any of our swimming excursions because he had to work at the cleaners.

My mother, always the adventurer and progressive in her thinking, upon learning of the Heman Park Swimming Pool, made plans to take us there. Since Olympia, at that time was the main driver of Henry, my mother would pile all of us into the car. Platon, Johnny and I in the back; my mother sitting in the front on the passenger side, with Olympia driving the car; and away we would go to Heman Park. Olympia would drive south for a block and a half on Aubert Avenue to Delmar Boulevard. Then she would turn right, and drive about four miles to University City. The entrance to the city was quite impressive. The City Hall, a circular building, was entered by stairs that were guarded by two stone lions. Driving on, it was a short distance to the park. For us, going to Heman Park made us feel that we were on a comparable financial level with the residents of University City.

The pool was spacious and outdoors. All of us would love to jump into the pool from the side, not bothering to walk down the three steps into the water. Jumping in was more adventurous, daring, and, for me, I was eager to let others see how brave I was!

Of course, we usually played in the shallow water because none of us really knew how to swim. Platon and Johnny, more daring than my sister and me, occasionally made forays into the deep water. My mother even had on a bathing suit, and would join us in the water. She knew how to swim, and would attempt to teach us the side stroke. On several occasions Platon's godmother, Kiki, joined us, with her special male friend. Kiki's husband was working at his barber shop. Another friend who joined us was Annie Belesot.

Johnny recalls that years later the St. Nicholas Church Sunday School had a picnic at the Heman Park Pool. Dessie our cousin was a year older than Johnny. Dessie was being chased by several boys, who tried to duck her in the water. She in turn thought it would be a good idea to duck Johnny in the water. He says she did manage to duck him.

He was surprised, and said to her, "Why did you do that?"

Our family enjoyed swimming at Heman Park for many summers, but in the meantime we had heard of another suburban swimming pool, further away in St. Louis County. One of Platon's friends, Leo Smith, told him about the pool. It was a mineral swimming pool in Meramec Valley.

Meramec Valley was about an hour's drive away from our home. It had a small river, the Meramec River, running through it, and the valley itself was composed of low lying hills. Many residents had homes built on the banks of the river, and I recall many of the homes were built on stilts. Occasionally, however, the river would flood and overrun it's banks, and the home owners found themselves with a serious problem. The Meramec River was not acceptable as a good place to swim, because it had many underwater currents.

My mother, ever on the watch to give her children pleasurable activities within her ability, got the directions to the Meramec Valley Swimming Pool. Again, Olympia was the designated driver, with Platon, Johnny and me in the back seat, and my mother seated in the front on the passenger side. Olympia would drive down Aubert Avenue south to the corner, turn right at Enright Avenue for a short block to Kingshighway Boulevard. Then she would go left, and drive for about fifteen miles south to Gravois Boulevard. From there she would go right until we reached Meramec Valley.

Of course, the drive to this pool took longer, but not one of us minded the distance since we were in the country and could enjoy scenery we did not see often. Farms, corn stalks swaying in the breeze, horses grazing in the fields, cows gathered around rolls of straw, chewing their cud.

The pool was not very crowded. It was not as nice as the pool in Heman Park. It was smaller but our family liked it. The pool had mineral water, a new experience for us.

We all enjoyed swimming in the mineral water. It was a fun day for us, but to our dismay, we found out when we went home that we were thoroughly exhausted. We were so tired that none of us ate anything, and without exception, we all went straight to bed and slept for several hours. We surmised that the minerals in the water had some kind of effect on the body, which made everyone so tired.

Johnny and Platon remember that our mother had a problem in the water there. She knew how to swim, there was no question. She was in the deep water, and suddenly started calling for help. Several people went to her aid, and she was helped out of the water.

Our family enjoyed swimming at Meramec Valley although we did not frequent it as often as we did Heman Park. Recalling those swimming trips to Meramec Valley, I think we all looked upon it as a summer adventure. Again, my father never came with us on our visits to Meramec Valley.

Henry had been a good transportation friend ... reliable; never giving us a problem; ready, willing and able to take us anywhere we desired. Olympia, too, was considerate, gracious, ever willing to please her siblings and mother by being a responsible and pleasant driver. As I recall, my siblings and I never quarreled or argued about anything. It seemed so natural to be going for an outing, and everyone getting along with each other. Looking back upon those swimming times, they were happy, convivial family outings.

Johnny recalls, years later, that he once went swimming in the downtown YMCA. He never went back again, because to his dismay, the boys were swimming without any suits, just naked. He did not care for that situation.

By now, the Thirties were gone, and the Forties came in, and the Depression was over!

In front of the backyard grape arbor, 1941.

Picnics

The Washington Elementary School picnic was held every year in June at the Forest Park Highlands on Oakland Avenue and Hampton Boulevard, next to the Arena. It was one of the most important school days for us, because it signaled that the end of the school year was approaching. It was a day full of fun and excitement, an opportunity to go to an amusement park and spend the entire day there. All my siblings and I, all the years we were students at Washington School, attended those picnics. My mother always made it a point to let her children attend that important school event. Our other Greek friends were just as excited as we were to go to the picnic.

For weeks before the school picnic, my Greek girlfriends and I would talk about the picnic constantly, the clothes we would wear on that day, the different rides we would go on, etc. We also talked about trying to save money to spend at the Highlands, but none of us got an allowance or had any way of getting any extra money. The Greek boys were able to get some money, they would go around looking for empty soda bottles to return to the store and get a penny for each one.

It was unthinkable for us to ask our parents for money to spend on rides or refreshments because during the Thirties, money was tight for almost everyone. However, my mother was generous to us on that day; she did give us money to spend on a few extra rides.

The morning of the picnic was an exciting one for us. We couldn't wait to leave the house to go to school, urging our siblings to "Hurry up, hurry up, let's go". We would grab the picnic basket my mother had made up, filled with hot dogs, buns, and other food, and off we would go to school.

Members of the Mother's Club and PTA comprised the Picnic Committee. They would charter buses to drive the students out to the grounds. The buses were double decker ones, and it was a treat to be able to sit in the upper deck, and look down at the people standing on the outside. Sometimes looking down from that height made me momentarily dizzy; nevertheless, it was exciting. The organizers of the picnic would accommodate the parents by checking the picnic baskets on the bus to be reclaimed at the Highlands. No accommodation was provided by the Picnic Committee for our transportation home, we each were on our own.

To return home after the picnic, it was every man for himself.

Parents were not allowed to ride the buses; they furnished their own transportation to the amusement park. With so many Greek families living on Aubert Avenue, there were many mothers of our Greek friends going to the school picnic too. My mother, and any small child she happened to have at the time who was not enrolled in school, as well as the other mothers, would walk down Aubert Avenue going south one block to Enright Avenue, turn right one block west to Kingshighway Boulevard. They would then board the Kingshighway bus going south to Oakland Avenue, then transfer to the Forest Park streetcar going west to the Forest Park Highlands.

At the school, there was no parade, no band, we simply boarded the buses by room assignment, and left. The buses would arrive at the Highlands before the mothers who were coming by public transportation. As we got off the chartered buses, we got our family's picnic basket and we would make a mad dash for the pavilion to find an empty table and hold it until our mother would come. The pavilion was an ideal place for the mothers to sit during the day while their children were enjoying themselves; they could visit with each other. The pavilion was sheltered, in case of rain or from the sunshine, and it was located almost in the middle of the amusement grounds. The Highlands had a swimming pool, but we never swam in it. There was also a ballroom dance area that opened at eight o'clock in the evening for dancing.

The children were given a certain number of free tickets, much coveted, from the Picnic Committee for the rides. We relied heavily on those. They were already stamped with the name of the ride they were good for. One was the Merry-Go-Round, one was for the Airplane Swing, and another was for the Racing Derby. For some of us, particularly the girls, the Racing Derby was too dangerous and challenging. We were usually able to trade that ticket with the boys for a Merry-Go-Round ticket (but never for an Airplane Swing because the boys liked the challenge that ride presented and kept the ticket for themselves).

My sister and I had devised our own plan for going on the rides. We would begin with the Merry-Go-Round, to get the feeling of the air brushing us as the Carousal was in motion. We sat on decorated wooden horses that bounced up and down, a good feeling of joy and being carefree. Then we would approach the Airplane Swing ride cautiously because that ride was a little livelier and more intimidating. It wasn't that we didn't want to ride it but the airplane lifted off the ground and swung out into the air at a little bit of an angle. However, we quickly overcame our fear of the obvious, and valiantly stood in line to get on the ride. Next we went to the Dodgem Cars. It was one of our favorite rides and we really enjoyed it. We had the feeling that we were actually driving an automobile, pressing our foot on the accelerator, careful not to hit other cars, moving the steering wheel back and forth, and then, deliberately hitting someone with the thought of teasing them, yelling at each other in fun and screaming. It was great fun.

Another ride that was intimidating to us was the Ferris Wheel. The seats were attached on different spokes of the Wheel and they did not lay flat; the Wheel was upright as it turned around. The height of the Wheel was equal perhaps to that of the third floor of a house. The seats rocked back and forth as the Wheel went around. There was a great deal of apprehension that, if the Wheel stopped to let someone off while we were at the very top of it, we were really in trouble with the seat rocking back and forth amid our screams of laughter. Fortunately there was a smaller Ferris Wheel, that did not reach very high, and the seats were enclosed in a cage. Even though there was the threat of being called a baby if one went on that Wheel, we took the challenge and did not hesitate, and rode it.

Sometime in the early afternoon the Picnic Committee had organized games for the children. We would all gather round and enjoy watching the different contests. One contest was that each contestant would stand in a gunny sack, and at the signal, hop to the end of a designated area. The first child to reach that spot was the winner. We never participated in any of the games, we were too self-conscious that we would lose.

By late afternoon, we had used up all our tickets and gone on the other rides with the money our mother gave us. We were getting tired, however not enough to leave the Highlands that early! Other students and parents began leaving the amusement park, but we would not budge. We still wanted to stay a little longer.

All the Greek mothers would stay at the picnic until it got dark, about nine o'clock in the evening; and then tired but enormously satisfied, the group of Greek mothers and children got ready to go home. Then we would all board the Forest Park streetcar going east and ride to Kingshighway Boulevard, take the Kingshighway bus going north to Enright Avenue, get off, walk one block east to Aubert Avenue, turn left and go home, weary, exhausted, but extremely happy.

Ready to jump the gates of the Municipal Opera, 1937.

Muny Opera

In the impressionable years of adolescence growing up in St. Louis in the thirties, one of the most enjoyable activities I recall fondly was in the summer attending the Municipal Theater. It is commonly referred to as the Muny Opera. Going to the Muny Opera in Forest Park was one of the highlights of the season for my siblings, for the Greek American children on Aubert Avenue, and for me.

The Muny Opera is an amphitheater set on the side of a hill, reminiscent of ancient Greek theaters. The theater was established in 1919, and seats over eleven thousand people. The stage was huge, and at that time, at each end of it was a large-branched, leafy tree. Since there were no curtains on the stage to hide the workmen changing the scenery, we were always fascinated by the method that accomplished that task. In the center of the stage, there was a revolving section that was turned by a machine hidden below the stage. Thus a change of scenery was achieved very quickly and efficiently.

Light opera productions and Broadway musicals were prominently featured with the leading roles played by nationally known stars of the theater. The rest of the cast was local talent. The presentations were accompanied by a full orchestra. Each week there was a new offering, and among them favorites like the Desert Song, Naughty Marietta, Gypsy, Show Boat and others. The Muny Opera operated from mid-June through August. We rarely missed a performance.

Our group from Aubert Avenue was made up of about ten to twelve young-sters, boys and girls, from the ages of eight to sixteen. The girls always wore a dress, which was the appropriate attire for those years, regardless of ethnic back-ground. Shorts or pants were not available for the female gender. No one of our sex even possessed such an article of clothing. The boys always wore long legged pants.

We would assemble at a prearranged time in front of someone's house in the early afternoon for our half hour walk to the Muny Opera. We would always walk the three miles to the theater; we had no other transportation. To go by bus was out of the question since most of the parents couldn't afford the expense. With the exception of my parents and one other family, no other Greek family on Aubert Avenue owned a car. Actually, we enjoyed walking to the Muny Opera, because there were interesting and beautiful things to see on the way.

Our itinerary would start with a walk south down Aubert Avenue to Delmar Avenue, turn right, go a block to Kingshighway Boulevard, and turn left. This was the beginning of an area of private streets and luxury apartment buildings and also, outstanding religious architecture. Walking through this area made us feel special, to feel we could be near homes and religious buildings where the upper middle class and wealthy people of St. Louis lived and worshiped. The residents belonged to elite clubs, owned automobiles, had servants do their housework and gardening, and sent their children to private schools like Mary Institute, Smith Academy, and City House.

As we walked down Kingshighway Boulevard, we would pass the Holy Corners at Washington Avenue. On each corner was a religious building. On the northwest side, was Temple Israel. On the same side of the street, on the southwest corner, was St. John's Methodist Church. Directly across the street, on the southeast corner was the Second Baptist Church. Going to the next block, we would wonder about the building that was occupied by a private men's club, called the Racquet Club. We would stare at the valet who stood at attention by the driveway to assist members entering or leaving the building, wondering which of these men were the ones who controlled the future of the city in their hands. Which of these men were the Buschs, Danforths, and other wealthy men of our community?

Continuing our walk, immediately adjacent to the Racquet Club, and for about a mile, were private streets on both sides of Kingshighway Boulevard, sheltering the large, magnificent homes of wealthy owners. Needless to say, we were very impressed by them, gawking at structures built in the 1890's, as we went by. How to compare those homes with the brick two-family flats we lived in on Aubert Avenue?

From there it was a short distance to the entrance of our beloved Forest Park. On June 24, 1876, the year our nation celebrated its centennial anniversary, at a large public ceremony, Forest Park was dedicated. It consisted of 1,370 acres, and today it is still one of the largest urban parks in the country. The park was originally four miles outside of the city limits, but by the Thirties the city had grown so much it enveloped the park.

Since it was still early afternoon, our group would head for the Pavilion, which was about a mile further inside Forest Park.

The Pavilion had been built in 1909 as a gift to the city from the 1904 World's Fair Board of Directors. It sat high on top of Government Hill overlooking a fountain that shot straight streams of water very high into the air. We loved to sit and attempt to guess how high the streams of water went. The older members of our group hazarded several guesses, and those of us who were younger would respectfully agree on the estimates. On particularly humid days, we would venture close to the base of the fountain, and run back and forth through the sprays of water, hoping to get some liquid relief from the heat. There was a shelter and refreshment stand at the Pavilion but none of us had any money to patronize it. The Pavilion was a favorite sight of my parents when we would go to Forest Park.

Across the road were picnic tables, and although as a rule none of us would bring any food with us, there were rare occasions when we did pack a picnic lunch. We usually assembled there.

Two things the boys were sure to bring with them were a stick and a cork ball, for playing cork ball. Both boys and girls made up the two teams. Playing cork ball with the boys was a treat for the girls because cork ball was the boy's domain. Waiting around to get into the Muny Opera to get free seats was the only time the boys would condescend and allow girls to play on their teams. We played cork ball in the afternoon until about six o'clock.

By then the group had had enough of the game of cork ball so we would walk the short distance through the park to the Muny Opera Theater. The management had a policy, in existence to this day, of allotting about ten rows in the back of the theater as free seats to the public. Since the performance was to begin at eight o'clock, the gates would be locked with a padlock and chain. Undaunted by this obstacle, one by one we would climb over the iron gate, giving assistance to those who had difficulty scaling the locked gate. Even though the girls wore dresses, climbing over the gate posed no problem.

At that early hour, our group were the only ones there, so we joyously scrambled over the seats, picking and choosing where we wanted to sit. We each had a front row seat right by the fence separating the free seats from the reserved paid seats. Our group was thrilled to be sitting in the free seats in the back of the amphitheater, and with anticipation and excitement were prepared to wait for the evening's performance.

Oftentimes, we were fortunate to witness the rehearsal of the forthcoming week's performance. We would scrutinize the actors on the stage, hoping to recognize and catch a glimpse of a well-known stage or screen personality. Some of us would softly shriek and giggle when we thought we saw a famous celebrity. It was interesting to see how the actor's rehearsed their roles.

At seven o'clock the iron gates would be unlocked, the ushers would take their places by the appropriate entrance, and the patrons would start to arrive.

Attending the Muny Opera was enchanting. We were transported to different worlds by the action on the stage, and saw behavior and life very different from what we knew or, at our age, had ever dreamed existed. The music of the Desert Song took us to the sands of another country and continent. Naughty Marietta took us to Europe as we watched the actors show us life in the 1800s. Each light opera was a cultural awakening for our group, one that broadened our intellectual capacities and made us aware of life in other places. These were wonderful cultural experiences.

About eleven o'clock, when the performance was over, tired but excited from the day's activities, our little group would assemble again in front of the theater, and start on our walk home to Aubert Avenue. Even though it was dark and we would have to go through Forest Park, to Kingshighway Boulevard, north to Delmar Boulevard to Aubert Avenue; past the private streets with the wealthy homes; past the Men's Club; past the Holy Corners, we had no thought of being afraid. Many people leaving the theater to go home were walking, or in cars, in the park, and on the busy streets.

Some of the girls would sing songs we had heard that evening; some of us would discuss the show and talk about the actors we had seen. We would arrive to our homes safe, if exhausted, but very happy, invigorated, thrilled with our attendance at the Muny Opera.

Nerazakia

The memory of the tangy taste and image of wild orange preserves comes instantly to my mind when I eat orange marmalade that I buy from the supermarket. The orange marmalade reminds me of the delicious preserves my mother used to make from wild oranges, which she called nerazakia, so many years ago. The nerazakia were slightly different in texture and composition from the orange marmalade I now get, but the taste is basically the same.

My mother's sister, Katina, lived in Phoenix, Arizona. Thea Katina's property was several acres in size with many citrus trees on it, grapefruit and orange trees. The orange trees were wild; they were not cultivated. The fruit could not be eaten when ripe. However, the oranges did have a specific use, they were great for making nerazakia, or wild orange preserves. Evidently, nerazakia were a Smyrnaiko delicacy familiar to anyone who had lived in Asia Minor. They were certainly a favorite of my parents' and my aunt's.

For as many years as I can remember, each season when the fruit ripened on the trees, thea Katina would send several boxes of the wild oranges to my mother. There were two kinds: the mature, ripened wild orange and the small, golf-ball sized, unripe green orange. My mother would make preserves from both kinds of oranges but my favorite preserve was from the large, ripe wild orange.

My mother inevitably looked forward to receiving the wild oranges. She would exclaim with pleasure, "Katina has remembered us again!" However, when I would see the boxes of fruit arrive, I would groan because I knew I would be a part of the crew that prepared the preserves. The process of cooking the large, ripe wild orange preserves was a tedious one, albeit the results were well worth the effort.

First the fruit was rinsed. Then the outside of each orange was scraped against the teeth of a cheese grater to rid the rind of the fruit of the orange color, until the white of the skin showed. This could be a hazardous operation; a person could inadvertently scrape the skin off their fingers! I learned quickly to apply myself as a conscientious and careful worker, to observe carefully what I was doing! Next, the rind was cut in strips, oval in shape, from the top of the orange to the bottom, about a half inch thick at its widest part. Then each piece of rind was rolled up and secured by a toothpick. The meat of the orange was discarded.

The next step was boiling the rolled up pieces of rind in water. Nothing else was added to the pot. They were boiled in a large pot for an hour. The water was discarded. Fresh water was put in the pot and the pieces of rind were boiled again for another hour. My mother used to say, "The oranges need to go through two boilings".

For the rest of the family, this step was a memorable one because the scent of the oranges was so overpowering and unpleasant. The memory and smell lingered in the house and in our noses for many days after.

The final step was in boiling the rinds again, this time with sugar. After that, the nerazakia were ready. The toothpick that had been inserted in each piece of rind to roll it up, was removed from the preserves. My mother would have clean Mason jars, and fill them with nerazakia. She would easily fill at least twenty jars and place them in the dining room, temporarily, because there was no room to store them in the kitchen. Jars of nerazakia would be placed on the sideboard in the dining room. The remaining jars were placed on the sills of the two windows, even behind the drapes. Now my mother had the task of determining to whom she would present as gifts the jars of wild orange preserves!

The nerazakia were a big hit with all our friends and neighbors, and even with guests who came to our home, particularly when we celebrated my father's Name Day, St. Stefan's Day, on December 27.

In the traditional Greek fashion, my mother would prepare the silver serving tray, placing a hand embroidered doily in the center of it. On it she would place the silver cup that held the spoons. In addition, there was a small silver dish with as many pieces of nerazakia as necessary to accommodate the number of guests, and several glasses of water.

The silver cup with the spoons and the silver dish had a special meaning for our family, because they were part of a small bundle of items that our paternal grandmother was able to save when she fled her home from the Turks and became a refugee in 1922 during the Catastrophe of Asia Minor, the burning of Smyrna. She had been found wandering and dazed in the burning city, clutching her precious bundle, by family friends and rescued.

It was our custom, when my sister and I became teenagers, to serve the guests. It was a social responsibility that we took seriously, to serve the older guests first, then the women, and then the men. For us, our father's Name Day was an important occasion, once every year, we respected the event and behaved accordingly.

Our Greek guests knew it was customary and the polite thing to do, to take one piece of nerazaki; that was sufficient. However, one afternoon someone who was not Greek came to our home on legal business. As was customary to show hospitality to a stranger, my mother prepared the silver tray with the doily, silver cup and spoons, the silver dish with about five pieces of nerazakia, and a glass of water. My mother instructed me to take the prepared tray and serve our guest. I did. I took the tray into the living room with my mother following me, and offered our guest the refreshments.

He smiled at me, profusely thanked my mother, and proceeded to take the silver dish with the five nerazakia off the tray, picked a spoon from the silver cup, and started to eat the preserves. He ate all of them! He was not aware of the fact he was supposed to take just one piece of the preserves! He drank the glass of water, and continued with the business he had come for.

Although I have never learned the technique of preparing and making nerazakia, suffice it to say the preserves the supermarket sells are enough to stir sweet memories for me, from a happy and distant past.

Pi Epsilon Pi, Washinton University's Greek American club, 1945.

College

The mailman has just delivered a copy of the Washington University in St. Louis Alumni Magazine. I'm always pleased to receive news of my alma mater, although it has been many years since I strolled down its tree shaded walks, hurrying to class from one ivy covered building to another. Crossing the Quadrangle to Ridgely Library, Eads Hall, Rebstock Hall, and Graham Chapel with its Gothic spires reaching for the sky, reminders of collegiate Gothic architecture. Happy, pleasant memories of long ago.

But, I think of a scene that took place before I compromised my original desire of the college of my choice.

"No, it cannot be done. You cannot go out of town to college," my mother said to me as we sat across from each other at the kitchen table. We were discussing a college for me to attend. My father was not present since he and my mother had already discussed the matter between them and reached an agreement. It was up to my mother now to do the negotiating.

"But mom, I want to be a journalist," I said looking into my mother's striking hazel green eyes. "Missouri University has one of the best Schools of Journalism in the country. Columbia is only one hundred miles away. My friends Edagrace and Romana are going. I really want to go there," I earnestly pleaded.

"No, Jennie, you will go to college in St. Louis," she answered in her kind but firm manner. "We have good schools here. You will also be helping at the cleaners. This way, you will help yourself and the family. We are family, and that is first and foremost."

"I don't want to stay in St. Louis," I protested. I felt like slamming my hands on the table, for emphasis but I knew it was useless. Theatrics or temper tantrums would be of no avail. They would be completely ignored. "Missouri University is the best. I want to be a journalist. That's where I should study," I petulantly responded.

"Jennie, in a family everyone must work together," my mother answered patiently. "Each person does not pull in his own direction. We must work together, for the good of all members of the family. We each cannot go our separate ways, we are one. For your good, and the good of the family. You will go to school in St. Louis, and help at the cleaners. That is all." With that final declaration, my mother rose from the table and left the room. The discussion was closed. No yelling, no loud voices, the discussion was over.

I went to the bedroom I shared with my sister. From the knotty pine desk drawer I pulled out all my old copies of my high school newspaper, The Griffin. I had not been an editor, just a reporter. I looked at the articles I had written. They really weren't much, basically two to three paragraph articles, for it was only a four page paper. But to me, as I reread what I had written, they were great.

I reached into the desk drawer again and took out the copy of the school yearbook, The Brochure. I was fortunate, to my way of thinking, to get my story, Was It To Be?, accepted for publication. In my enthusiasm, I thought the title was provocative, and in keeping with current events. The story dealt with the Nazi air bombing over England during World War II. I felt I had a certain knack for writing, and with the publication of my story, I felt I had arrived as a writer. The political events in Europe had fired up my imagination. I avidly read the St. Louis Post Dispatch, for news of the war, with dispatches from the front by Ernie Pyle, who traveled with the American troops, and Dorothy Thompson, who was stationed in England. Edward R. Morrow, Eric Sevareid, H. V. Kaltenborn—unforgettable names in broadcast journalism. Theirs was adventure, theirs was life.

I had set my sights on Mizzou. The only problem with that desire was that, in those years, very rarely was a Greek American girl allowed to go to an out-of-town university. A boy would be allowed to do so but a girl was considered sheltered and inexperienced with the world. She needed protection, for she could be vulnerable to the temptations of life.

There was also another problem. I had to work at the family business, the cleaners. The cleaners was doing a brisk business, due in part to the fact that besides my parents working there, as each child reached the age of twelve, he/she worked part time as called upon. My parents already had educated one child, my sister Olympia, and besides me, there would be two younger brothers to follow.

And so it was that I stayed in St. Louis and attended Washington University. But after my first semester there, my regret that I wasn't allowed to attend my first choice began to dim.

During my years at Washington University, because of the war and so many of the young men in service, it was like a girls school. The faculty was good, the classes small, and the campus beautiful, spread over one hundred sixty-nine acres. Some of the buildings had originally been a part of the 1904 World's Fair. To me, it was almost a fantasy world, removed from reality.

As the beginning of a new semester approached, many times over the four years, I vividly recall my father, on a Saturday night standing at the elaborate scroll-patterned National Cash Register with his gray head bent, counting the day's receipts. We had closed the store, I was getting my things together for us to go home, my mother was still at the sewing machine putting her work items away. With pencil in hand, studying the figures he had written he would ask the same question of my mother, "How much money does Jennie need for the tuition on Monday for Washington University?"

My mother's answer would invariably be, "Well, the tuition this semester is $125.00. She'll need about $25 for the different fees, and her books. Give her $150."

He would answer, in his gentle manner, for he very much believed in education for his children, "All right, in that case, we'll leave several bills unpaid so she can have the money for this semester." Then he would enumerate which bills he would pay and which bills he would temporarily let go.

On Monday morning, I would board the Kingshighway bus going south, transfer to the Maryland Avenue street car going west, clutching my purse that contained the cash my father had given me. I would get off at the Washington University stop. I would walk into the Registrar's Office in Brookings Hall and pay my tuition for the semester.

I was an average student. Never once did my parents question my grades, good or bad. To them I always did well. Actually I attended college because of my parents' unselfish love for me and their belief in my ability. Perhaps if I could have devoted more time to studying I could have gotten better grades; but as soon as my classes at the university were over for the day, I had to leave the school and go to the cleaners to work until closing time at nine o'clock and then go home to study. That daily arrangement, work and school, was difficult for me. However, my parents never questioned my grades, never chastised me for them, never said an unkind word to me about them. They always encouraged me.

On several occasions my mother would reinforce my scholastic endeavors by saying, "Education is a bracelet no one can take away from you." I bless my wonderful parents for their love and faith in me and for encouraging me to continue my education.

I still remember my parents' joy the day I graduated from Washington University. The pride in my father's eyes, the beaming smile on his face. The tears in my mother's eyes, the embrace of happiness she gave me.

Compromises must invariably be made in life. I loved Washington University, even though over the years on occasion there was some regret that I didn't realize my dream of being a journalist. Other interests developed in my life: marriage, raising a family, being of service to others through teaching. Those are values I believe one can be proud of, and they are evidence of a fulfilling life.

As my daughter Evangeline and son Elias were growing up, we had many occasions to drive by Washington University. Invariably I would remark to them, "Now, when you ...," and literally a Greek chorus would respond from the back of the car, "... are ready for college, you will come to Washington University like your mother!"

And without any question, they did!

Washington University Graduation Day, June 13, 1946

Epilogue

My Greek Ameican Sanctuary is now gone but the memories remain strong and vivid to this day. Gone is the house at 761 Aubert Avenue; only the lot remains. Gone are the three mulberry trees in the front yard, the grape arbor in the backyard and the cherry tree that endured countless assaults from my brothers. Gone are the rose bushes my father had planted along the sidewalk and the Chinese elm tree that Platon received on Arbor Day from school and planted. It was just a sapling, but Platon nurtured it and by the time we left Aubert Avenue it had grown to a considerable height.

Where is the wide front porch where I spent so many summer afternoons playing Monopoly, watching and listening with childish anticipation for the arrival of Tony the ice-cream man in his white horse-drawn cart? It is said that nothing is so constant as change, but the happy, nostalgic memories are so deeply etched in my mind they will never be erased. I am grateful that I was fortunate to be blessed with loving and supportive parents and siblings; with an ethnic community that gave me self-confidence, security, understanding. It is because I cherish them that I wrote these stories.

A Letter to Her Father

Perhaps the strings of her own mortality were pulling strongly that when Jennie Vlanton sat down at her personal computer and wrote a letter to her father. Stefanos Constantinides had died more than half a century earlier, but his daughter, herself at the end of the journey, remembered her father's sacrifices and legacy.

July, 2005

Dear Dad,

Your little girl is now 81 years old, and my nest has emptied. My children, now adults, are carving their own paths in the world. In my golden years, memories of you and mom are ever present. Wasn't it only yesterday that we were living in St. Louis, along with my brothers and sister, trying to survive the Depression? Although gone for 55 years, you, dad, are everywhere in my life.

I think of your life in this country, how you and mom came to the United States in 1919, from Smyrna, [now Izmir], Asia Minor. You were on your honeymoon. Your intent was to visit mom's sister and two brothers in St. Louis, then return to Smyrna. However, catastrophic political circumstances that erupted thousands of miles away sealed your fate and the United States became your home.

I especially recall the early Thirties, the years of the Depression, and the lesson I learned from you about family. Family values and unity of family. There was an unspoken feeling of the members of the family sharing a common goal, the solidarity of the family; without ever expressing it in words, you showed it by example, focusing all your energies into that one goal, family. How did I learn this lesson? Even though you never expressed that thought in words, you set the example.

I realize now that because of your devotion, we had a family life strengthened by love, unity, traditions and customs. I recall the dry cleaning and hat blocking business you had [Progressive Hatters and Cleaners]. Each of us, my three siblings and I, were called upon to work at the cleaners when business was brisk. You demonstrated by your behavior that you were a kind, compassionate, mild-mannered man; a man of refinement, not vulgar. You never struck, insulted or reprimanded any of your children. Through all the years we each worked at the cleaners you never yelled or corrected us, or said anything cross or embarrassed us.

The cleaners is still in the family today, run by your son, my brother.

As far back as I can remember, from a child to the day you passed away, you worked thirteen hours a day, opening the cleaners promptly at eight o' clock on the morning and closing at nine in the evening. That was during the week and on Saturdays, and on Sundays the store was open from nine in the morning to one o'clock in the afternoon. I cannot recall that you ever complained of the long hours.

During the dark and difficult days of the Depression business was very slow. You couldn't afford to hire any help; you did all the work in the store yourself. You shined customer's shoes, cleaned and blocked hats, pressed the clothes. I recall the endless hours you put in of hard work, and of your sacrifices.

Remember the shoe shine stand, how a customer had to step up to the marble stand to sit in the chair, then place his feet on the brass foot pedestals to get his shoes shined?

Shining shoes is honorable work, but to my young mind, it presented another picture. How many times I felt sad watching you shine the shoes of a customer who was sitting in the chair, with his feet on the foot rests. Your duty, your responsibility were clear to you. There was no question in your mind about your role. You did it willingly and happily because it sustained and nurtured your family.

And yet I never heard you gripe about shining shoes, or the long hours you were putting in at the cleaners. When you got home from the store at nine-thirty in the evening, you would eat dinner. You would stay up for about an hour and then go to bed. The next morning when you got up, I recall, you were always in a good mood.

I admire you for the kind, compassionate, mild mannered man you were, and that you never grumbled of the long hours you worked.

I recall the store directly across the street from our cleaners, the one with the name, "Sam The Tailor" posted across the plate glass window. It was operated by a husband and wife. Sam basically did tailoring, but he also took in dry cleaning and hats.

Sam also closed at nine o' clock at night. Dad, you were ever observant of Sam's movements. I recall when I was a teenager working at the cleaners, you would look across the street at Sam's and wait for him to close. You did that because if an individual went to Sam's with dry cleaning, or a hat needing cleaning and blocking, and Sam was closed, the customer would cross the street and come to our store. When there was no light in Sam's store, you would say: "Sam has turned out his lights. He has closed for the day. We can get ready to go home now too".

During the Depression, in the summer months that were traditionally slow periods in the dry cleaning business, there were many times we walked home from the cleaners. We did that because we did not have a car. The distance was three miles. All of us, you, and mom, who by then had convinced you to let her work at the cleaners doing the alterations, or any sibling or I who had been at the cleaners that day; we all walked home. We would leave the store a few minutes after nine o' clock, regardless of the thirteen hours you had put in at the cleaners, regardless of the heat and humidity that is found in St. Louis summer weather, we would walk home. You never whined about having to walk home, and as I recall, none of us did either. We just assumed that if you thought we should do it, it was the right thing to do. Again, you were setting an example of behavior for us.

Streetcar fares at the time were ten cents for adults and five cents for children twelve years of age or younger. That was a considerable amount of money in the period of the Depression. Ten cents would buy a loaf of bread, and if it was bread more than a day old, (it was called stale), a person could buy it for five cents. Never did I hear you express any word of discontent about walking home after working so many hours in the cleaners.

To you, the cleaners meant security, pride, independence. It gave you the satisfaction of knowing you were capable of providing for your family. You knew your family would have food, a roof over their heads, even during the worst period of the Depression. Your family would not need to go on Relief, which was the government program at the time to help destitute families; or to depend on handouts from others.

Dad, I remember your generosity, and the confidence you and mom had in me when I wanted to go to college. I enrolled at Washington University in St. Louis. This was the beginning of the Forties. Tuition was $250 a year. The national economy had improved considerably by then, although that amount of money was a lot for a small business owner to spend, for that time, on an expensive private college education.

As the beginning of a new semester approached, many times over the four years, I vividly recall you, on a Saturday night, standing at the elaborate scroll-patterned National Cash Register. Your head was bent down, counting the day's receipts. The store was closed, I was getting my things ready to go home, mom was still at the sewing machine putting her items away. With pencil in hand, studying the figures you had written on a piece of paper, you would ask mom the same question, How much money does Jennie need for tuition on Monday for Washington University?"

The answer would invariably be: "Well, the tuition this semester is $125. She'll need about $25 for the different fees, and her books. Give her $150."

You would answer in your gentle manner, for you very much believed in education for your children: "All right, in that case, we'll leave several bills unpaid so she can have the money for the tuition this semester." Then you would enumerate the bills you would pay, and which bills you would temporarily let go for a few weeks.

On Monday morning I would board the bus, transfer to the street car, clutching my purse that contained the cash you had given me. I did not have a check, just cash. I would get off at the Washington University stop. I would walk into the Registrar's office in Brookings Hall and pay my tuition for the semester.

Never once did you question my grades, good or bad. You always felt I did well. Actually I attended college because of your and mom's unselfish love and belief in my ability. You understood that I was doing my best, because as soon as my classes were over I would leave the university and come to the cleaners to work. I stayed until closing time at nine o' clock, and when we went home, I would study for my classes the next day. That daily arrangement, work and school, was difficult for me. You always encouraged me.

I bless you and mom for supporting me with your love and faith to continue my education, which resulted in my becoming an elementary school teacher.

Dad, I still remember your and mom's joy at the commencement exercises the day I graduated from Washington University. The pride in your eyes, the beaming smile on your face; mom's tears of joy.

I am grateful that I was fortunate to be blessed with a loving and supportive father and mother that gave me self-confidence, security, understanding.

I had the good fortune to have a father who was of good character, who had a strong work ethic, and religious beliefs that helped mold the life of my siblings and myself.

Your duty, your responsibility, were clear to you. There was no question in your mind about your role. You were the head of the family, this was the lifestyle for you. You did it willingly and happily because it sustained and nurtured your family.

You worked hard and strenuously to achieve an average way of life, and you surpassed it by your achievement; not only did our family survive, but it prospered.

Hopefully, I have been able to pass on these qualities to my own children, and on their part, to their children.

Your loving daughter,

Jennie

A Son's Eulogy

Jennie Constantinides Vlanton died on August 8, 2017. That same year, her youngest brother John and her older sister Olympia, also died. The following year her brother Platon died. So now the house and the family are gone, leaving only this book of Jennie's memories of one Greek immigrant family who came to St. Louis, Missouri, in the early years of the twentieth century.

At her funeral, her son Elias Vlanton captured the spirit of Jennie's life in the following eulogy.

A mother, a grandmother, a teacher, an author, and a historian, Jennie Constantinides Vlanton was all of these things. And she was, like all of us, a product of her time and place: a Greek immigrant daughter who grew up in the Great Depression, experienced the drama of World War II, embarked on a profession when many women were confined to domesticity, and who lived long enough to enjoy the fruits of her efforts, the success of her children and grandchildren.

Her sacrifice for her children and grandchildren knew few limits. Decades before cultural enrichment became fashionable for the upwardly mobile, my parents made sure Evangeline and I took piano lessons, signed up for the Baden Library summer reading programs, attended Saturday science classes, enjoyed matinees at the American Theater in downtown St. Louis, and evening summer performances at the Municipal Opera. During family vacations, my mother would not miss an opportunity to teach; explaining the significance of any historical landmark we crossed. She battled to give my sister and I the better things of life. My sister dreamed of attending Washington University, but senior year my father's pocketbook was set on a more frugal path, the community college. To break the deadlock, my mother sent the deposit to Washington University without informing my father. "Elia, I've worked for over a decade so my children could receive the same university education I had," she informed him "and Evangeline is going there."

The university education meant so much to my mother because she loved learning, and her creative mind found its full expression in her writing. Even as a young girl of 13, she kept a diary, one of the our prized possessions, and at age 16 she published her first short story titled "Was It To Be?" in the Blewett High

School yearbook. When I recently read it, about an English pilot shot down during the Nazi Blitz over London, the writing was so compelling I flipped back several times to confirm the story had my mother's byline.

Passionate on a range of issues, my mother wrote and delivered many speeches on Greek history and immigration to America to audiences in St. Louis and in Akron. As a 12-year-old I remember Nick Matsakis assigning her to speak at the Annunciation Church on Cyprus. She toiled over that manuscript and after being introduced she began nervously, hands shaking and voice unsteady. But her passion was so evident and her arguments so effective that after the third member spontaneously jumped up and shouted out "Bravo Jenny" I did not even have to wait until the standing ovation to know my mother had conquered.

Her great curiosity drove her to spend hours at research institutions, ranging from the Library of Congress, where she studied 16th century maps of Cerigo for evidence of her ancestral village, to the St. Louis Central Library, where she sat patiently at a microfilm machine, scanning newspapers for stories on the early Greeks in St. Louis. My sister's PhD. dissertation and my book on George Polk were immensely aided by her relentless pursuit of the arcane reference or forgotten article, as well as by her unqualified affirmation that yes, we were capable of achieving these goals. In her 80s, we told her that it was time to focus on her own writing and she rewarded us with her memoir *761 Aubert, My Greek American Sanctuary* a book-length memoir capturing her childhood on Aubert Avenue.

She was not a rebel by nature, but her deeply held beliefs were unbending. At Baden Elementary School in the 1970s, when the white teachers snubbed the newly arrived black teachers during lunch at the teacher's lounge, my mother stopped having lunch there and sat separately in a classroom with the black teachers. She did it because it was the right thing to do, she said, and—conveniently--she enjoyed their company more.

She also strongly believed in immigrants—regardless of where they came from or their legal status. When I was teaching I told her about a hard-working immigrant student of mine who was in college but had no means of support and asked if she could help. Every month for the next three years, until she graduated, my mother sent this young woman, whom she had never met, a $125 check—each check accompanied by my mother's words of encouragement.

And—clever that my mother was—she never told my father she was doing it.

Will I miss my mother? No, I won't. Why would I? At home, I am completing a dozen of her unfinished projects. Her memoir sits arms reach on my bookshelf. And six decades of memories provide endless comfort.

Memories. There are so many I can't remember them all! Even at the end, her wit did not fail. Caring for her with my sister in her final days I was unable to go out for food and started eating the only thing I could find in her room, stale cookies. My mom had been mumbling unintelligently throughout the day but as I bit down into my second chocolate chip I was startled to hear: "Who here is eating a cookie?" "Do you want some, mom?" I said. As I put a nibble in her mouth I asked if it was tasty, which earned a "mmmm;" after I fed the second piece I received a smile, before she returned to mumbling in her sleep.

The last memory was more poignant. When Evangeline and I returned Sunday morning, my sister began her morning ritual. "Elia, your son, and me, Evangeline, your daughter, are here to be with you, mom." By then she had completely lost the ability to speak or even mumble, but her lips formed a single word, one she had often used to express her joy: "wow". She knew who we were, that we were there, and she was happy. And that--the last word she spoke--really said it all.

How can I end this tribute? I find words no better than those my mother wrote in her epilogue to her memoir, when she tried to understand the meaning of the events long gone:

> My Greek American Sanctuary is now gone but the memories remain strong and vivid to this day. Gone is the house at 761 Aubert Avenue; only the lot remains. Gone are the three mulberry trees in the front yard, the grape arbor in the backyard and the cherry tree that endured countless assaults from my brothers. Gone are the rose bushes my father had planted along the sidewalk and the Chinese elm tree that Platon received on Arbor Day from school and planted. It was just a sapling, but Platon nurtured it and by the time we left Aubert Avenue it had grown to a considerable height.
>
> Where is the wide front porch where I spent so many summer afternoons playing Monopoly, watching and listening with childish anticipation for the arrival of Tony the ice-cream man in his white horse-drawn cart? It is said that nothing is so constant as change, but the happy, nostalgic memories are so deeply etched in my mind they will never be erased. I am grateful that I was fortunate to be blessed with loving and supportive parents and siblings; with an ethnic community that gave me self-confidence, security, understanding. It is because I cherish them that I wrote these stories.

Stefan and Evengelia, 1949.

A Note on Photographs

The photographs of Ellis Island, the shoe shine parlor, the streetcar and the dandelions are from the Library of Congress' Photographs and Prints Division. The shoe shine parlor photo was taken in 1908 (Call Number Lot 7480, v. 1, no. 0050), the Ellis Island photo was taken circa 1907–1921 (Call Number Lot 7172, item 97501087), and the streetcar photo was taken circa 1936 (Call Number LC-USF344-000838-ZB). The photo of the dandelions was Call Number LC-H823-2090-008.

All other photographs are in the private family collections of Jennie Constantinides Vlanton and Olympia Constantinides Glynias. The years given in the captions are approximate, based on the ages of those pictured and other details.

www.ingramcontent.com/pod-product-compliance
Lightning Source LLC
Chambersburg PA
CBHW020431290526

45785CB00002B/797